AMERICAN VOICES FROM

The Revolutionary War

The Battle of Lexington, April 19th 1775. Plate I.
1. Major Pitcairn at the head of the Regular Granadiers.
2. The Party who first fired on the Provincials at Lexington.
3. Part of the Provincial Company of Lexington.
4. Regular Companies on the road to Concord.
5. The Meetinghouse at Lexington.
6. The Public Inn.
A. Doolittle Sculp

AMERICAN VOICES FROM

The Revolutionary War

Susan Provost Beller

BENCHMARK BOOKS
MARSHALL CAVENDISH
NEW YORK

TO DARBY,
my Muse

Benchmark Books
Marshall Cavendish
99 White Plains Road
Tarrytown, New York 10591-9001
www.marshallcavendish.com

Map by Laszlo Kubinyi

Library of Congress Cataloging-in-Publication Data
Beller, Susan Provost, 1949–
The Revolutionary War / by Susan Provost Beller.
p. cm. — (American voices from—)
Summary: Presents the history of the American Revolution through excerpts from letters, newspaper articles, journal entries, and laws of the time.
Includes bibliographical references and index.
ISBN 0-7614-1202-6
1. United States—History—Revolution, 1775–1783—Juvenile literature.
2. United States—History—Revolution, 1775–1783—Sources—Juvenile literature. [1. United States—History—Revolution, 1775–1783—Sources.] I. Title. II. Series.
E208 .B45 2002 973.3—dc21
2001008741

Printed in Italy
1 3 5 6 4 2

Series design and composition by Anne Scatto / PIXEL PRESS
Photo Research by Anne Burns Images

Cover Photo: The Granger Collection.

The photographs in this book are used by permission and through the courtesy of:
The Granger Collection: ii, xxii, 10, 14, 24, 54, 60, 72, 77, 78, 91
The Colonial Williamsburg Foundation: viii, 3, 96(left bottom & right bottom), 97(bottom)
Hulton: xi, 26, 34, 37, 43, 48, 80
North Wind Pictures: xiv, 6, 20, 29, 46, 59, 63, 66, 75, 82, 85, 89, 97(upper)
Superstock: 32 Stock Montage
Art Resource: xii, 44 Scala, 69 Reunion des Musees Nationaux
Adams National Historic Park: 94 upper and lower

ON THE COVER: The American flag is raised as the British leave New York at war's end.

ON THE TITLE PAGE: An engraving of the Battle of Lexington, done shortly after the event by Connecticut militiaman Amos Doolittle.

Acknowledgments

The author is grateful to the staff of the Manuscript Division of the Library of Congress for their extensive assistance in locating sources that are usually overlooked by researchers and to the librarians at the Dana Medical Library of the University of Vermont for use of their collection of historical textbooks.

Contents

Williamsburg april 8th. 1772. I
Received from George Washington
the sum of seven pounds seven shil
and six pence in full of all acct.
to this date.

C Campbell

George Washington's receipt for his stay at a tavern in Williamsburg, Virginia, is a fine example of a primary source document.

About Primary Sources

What Is a Primary Source?

In the pages that follow, you will be hearing many different "voices" from a special time in America's past. Some of the selections are long and others short. You'll find many easy to understand, but some may require several readings. All the selections have one thing in common, however. They are primary sources. This is the name historians give to the pieces of information that make up the record of human existence. Primary sources are important to us because they are the very essence, the core material for all historical investigation. You could call them "history" itself.

Primary sources *are* evidence; they give historians all-important clues to understand the past. Perhaps you have read a detective story in which a sleuth has to solve a mystery by piecing together bits of evidence that he or she uncovers. The detective makes deductions, or educated guesses, based on the evidence, and solves the mystery once all the deductions point in a certain direction. Historians work in much the same way. Like detectives, historians analyze the data by careful reading and rereading. After much analysis, historians draw conclusions about an event, a person, or an entire era. Two historians may analyze the same evidence and come to different conclusions. This is why there is often sharp disagreement about an event.

Primary sources are also called *documents*—a rather dry word to describe what can be just about anything: an official speech by a government leader, an old map, an act of Congress, a letter worn out from too much handling, an entry hastily scrawled into a diary, a detailed newspaper account of a tragic event, a funny or sad song, a colorful poster, a cartoon, a faded photograph, or someone's eloquent remembrance captured on tape or film.

By examining the following primary sources, you, the reader, will be taking on the role of historian. Here is a chance to immerse yourself in an exciting era of American history—the Revolutionary War. You will come to know the voices of the men and women who created our country. You will read the words of soldiers and civilians, of political leaders, of allies who came to help to fight our cause. You will also read the words of those who fought against us and those among us who argued to remain loyal to the king.

Our language has changed since those early days. People were more formal in the way they wrote. Their everyday vocabulary contained words that will be unfamiliar to someone living in this century. Sometimes they spelled words differently, too. Don't be

Music for "Yankee Doodle," a patriotic song of the American Revolution

discouraged! Trying to figure out language is exactly the kind of work a historian does. Like a historian, when your work is done, you will have a deeper, more meaningful understanding of the past.

How to Read a Primary Source

Each document in this book deals with the Revolutionary War. Some of the documents are from government archives such as the Library of Congress. Others are from the official papers of major figures in American history. Many of the documents are taken from the letters, diaries, and reminiscences that ordinary people wrote. All of the documents, major and minor, help us to understand what it was like to be a part of the American Revolution.

As you read each document, ask yourself some basic but important questions. Who is writing? Who is the writer's audience? What is the writer's point of view? What is he or she trying to tell that audience? Is the message clearly expressed, or is it implied, that is, stated

This drawing of a Revolutionary War soldier can be found in the Free Library of Philadelphia.

indirectly? What words does the writer use to convey his or her message? Are the words emotion-filled or objective in tone? If you are looking at a painting, examine it carefully, taking in all the details. What's happening in the foreground? In the background? What message is the artist trying to express? These are questions that help you to think critically about a document.

Some tools have been included with the documents to help you in your historical investigations. Unusual words have been defined near the selections. Thought-provoking questions follow each document. They help focus your reading so you're able to get the most out of the document. As you read each selection, you'll probably come up with many questions of your own. That's great! The work of a historian always leads to many, many questions. Some can be answered, others cannot and require further investigation.

The fighting begins as the militia meet the British in Concord, Massachusetts, in April 1775.

Introduction

THE MOST AMAZING REVOLUTION

The most amazing fact about the American Revolution is that it ever took place. The second most amazing fact is that it was successful.

The thirteen colonies that went to war and won their independence from Great Britain began this war with little, if any, experience in warfare. They had no standing army, no navy, and little in the way of popular support. They faced the greatest empire in the world at that time. Great Britain had the most successful army in the world and the largest and most effective naval fleet in history. Great Britain had recently defeated the second biggest colonial empire, the French, in the Seven Years War. Great Britain also had the resources to purchase the services of additional troops, mercenaries known as Hessians from the German province of Hesse.

Great Britain also had history on its side. It was unheard of for a colony to win independence from its mother country. Some colonies, like New France (today's province of Quebec, Canada), had lost their ties to their mother country after being taken over by another colonial empire. But to actually revolt against the mother country, go to war, and win—this would be a major accomplishment indeed!

The colonies could not even call on the support of all of their residents. Historians estimate that only about one-third of the colonists were Patriots—active supporters of the independence movement. Another third were neutral in the fight—they wanted improved conditions and less taxation by the British government and the king, but they did not wish to go to war and were not active supporters of independence. The final third were the Tories or Loyalists, who strongly supported the British government. The Loyalists feared (and it was a justified fear) that rebellion against the king would only result in harsh retaliation and great suffering for the colonies. History and experience supported the Loyalist position. The British government had a long record of brutally suppressing rebellion in its colonies.

The one word that may best describe why the British lost the American colonies and why the colonists won their independence is stubbornness. The British legislature, called Parliament, and King George III stubbornly refused to listen to those who felt that some compromise with the colonies was necessary. Parliament was determined that the colonies would be governed by Britain and unwilling to allow the self-governance to which the colonists felt they were entitled. British leaders seemed insulted at the very thought of upstart colonials daring to question their power and their right to determine the future of the colonies.

What Parliament and the king did not realize is that they faced equal stubbornness on the part of the Patriots. Members of Parliament refused to address the original, rather mild, Patriot protests and reacted to the colonies with increased control and greater demands. They passed stricter legislation, levying taxes on items like tea and sugar. They even required the colonists to house and pay for the troops sent to prevent them from rebelling. The more they demanded, the more the colonists hardened their positions. What began as a formal request for redress of their grievances gradually became demands and finally recognition that their grievances would never be resolved. With that recognition a small group began to argue for the unthinkable: a declaration of separation from their mother country.

Those leading the fight in the colonies were willing to sacrifice everything for their freedom from Great Britain. They knew that if they failed, they would face death as traitors. A traitor's death under British law would be particularly gruesome. The victim was "hanged, drawn, and quartered." Parliament guessed wrong when it thought that no one would be willing to take that risk. But risk death the Patriots did. Amazingly, they won.

It did not look as if the Patriots had any hope of winning their fight for independence. From a military standpoint, after some early successes, the course of the war in the first few years was a near disaster for the colonial forces. The British had a simple strategy to suppress the rebellion. They would divide the Northern (or New England) Colonies where the most active rebellion was taking place, and then gradually return the other colonies to submission. The strongest base of Loyalist support was in the middle Atlantic area in New York, New Jersey, Pennsylvania, and Delaware. British troops would land in New York and then push inland. Additional British forces would embark from Montreal, Canada, and move south through the Champlain and Hudson valleys to meet the New York troops.

The colonists were able to stop the British advance from Canada through delaying tactics in 1776 and finally through the defeat of the British and Hessians at the Battle of Saratoga in 1777. George Washington and the Continental Army had also been successful in driving the British from Boston in March 1776.

When the British began their occupation of New York City in July 1776, the army under General Washington began a slow retreat in front of the British and Hessian regulars. His unprepared army of 20,000 men were facing 45,000 experienced soldiers. With his troops in tatters, Washington barely made it across the Delaware River to Pennsylvania in December 1776. Then he was finally able to fight back, attacking the Hessians by surprise at Trenton, New Jersey, the day after Christmas. The British advance continued in the Middle Colonies, and by late September 1777, they had occupied Philadelphia and held the two largest cities in the colonies.

In their stubbornness, the Patriots still held on. With the victory at Saratoga, they began to receive support from France and other European countries. By June 1778, with the Battle of Monmouth, they were able to bring the war to a stalemate in the Middle Colonies. The armies did not know it but the major fighting in that area was now over, although the British would not evacuate their troops from New York City until after the signing of the Treaty of Versailles in 1783.

The British next planned to take the Southern Colonies and then move northward. They took Savannah, Georgia, in 1779 and then Charleston, South Carolina (the fourth largest city in the colonies), in the spring of 1780. The Patriots' southern forces continually harassed the British troops, trying to avoid major battles, in which they were usually defeated. The British remained in control of the area, but it was a very weak control. Constant Patriot attacks

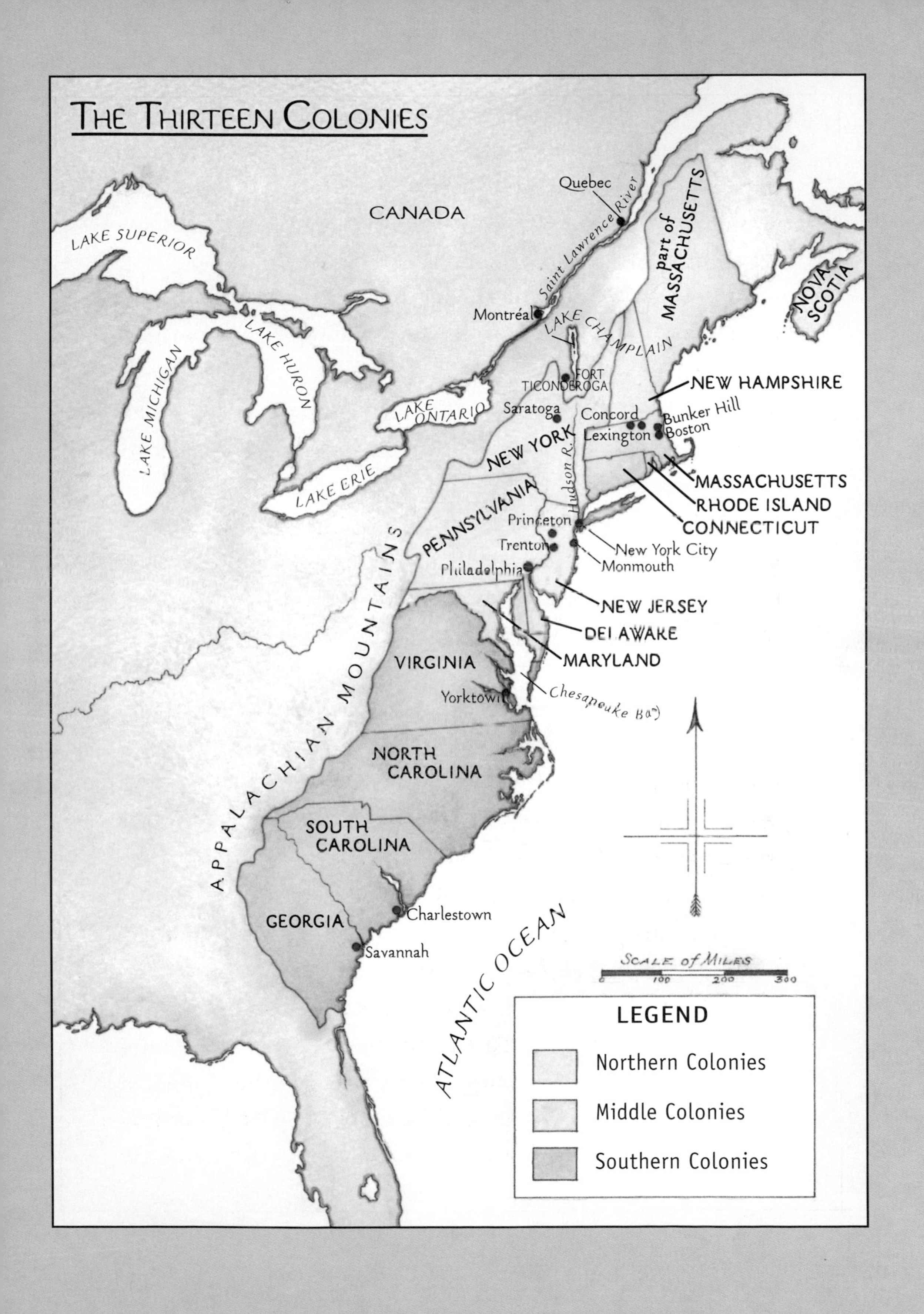
THE THIRTEEN COLONIES
CANADA
LAKE SUPERIOR
LAKE MICHIGAN
LAKE HURON
LAKE ONTARIO
LAKE ERIE
Quebec
Saint Lawrence River
Montréal
LAKE CHAMPLAIN
FORT TICONDEROGA
Saratoga
part of MASSACHUSETTS
NOVA SCOTIA
NEW HAMPSHIRE
Concord
Lexington
Bunker Hill
Boston
NEW YORK
Hudson R.
MASSACHUSETTS
RHODE ISLAND
CONNECTICUT
PENNSYLVANIA
Princeton
Trenton
Philadelphia
New York City
Monmouth
NEW JERSEY
DELAWARE
MARYLAND
VIRGINIA
Yorktown
Chesapeake Bay
APPALACHIAN MOUNTAINS
NORTH CAROLINA
SOUTH CAROLINA
GEORGIA
Charlestown
Savannah
ATLANTIC OCEAN
SCALE of MILES
0
100
200
300
LEGEND
Northern Colonies
Middle Colonies
Southern Colonies

were eroding their army. The southern strategy came to an end at Yorktown, Virginia, when British General Charles Cornwallis managed to get his army pinned with its back to the sea. A great cooperative effort by American and French soldiers, under the command of General Washington and the French general Jean-Baptiste Rochambeau, laid siege to Yorktown, while the French fleet prevented the British from escaping by sea. On October 19, 1781, Cornwallis surrendered his troops. The Revolutionary War was over even though the final peace treaty was still two years away.

With some understanding of the what and when of the events of the Revolutionary War, it is time to look at the conflict through several themes that can give us the perspective of the people who actually lived the experience.

The first two themes are the "why" of the war. This is the story of how the war came to be—a long process, beginning with Britain's need to pay off debt it had incurred during the Seven Years War. The road to war begins with Parliament's failure to consult with the colonists before levying taxes to raise the needed money. We'll consider this issue from both sides, first from the British and then from the colonists' perspective. This story of the developing conflict between Britain and the colonies, and among the colonists themselves, takes us to our third and fourth themes.

"Who" were these Patriots who took on the challenge of fighting the world's greatest army? The nature and character of the Patriots form the next two themes: becoming soldiers and the horrors of battle. Here the story of the war is viewed through the eyes of those who fought it. We see the hardships endured by these inexperienced and less-than-well-provisioned troops. We next follow them onto the battlefield as they become real soldiers. Finally we learn how the enemy perceived these Patriot soldiers.

Our fifth theme deals with a different "who"—women involved in the Revolutionary War. What was happening at home while the soldiers were fighting? What was it like to be in the path of war? What was it like to live behind enemy lines as a Patriot, or as a Loyalist trying to survive among the Patriots? What was it like to come to America as the wife of a Hessian soldier and spend the war in captivity with him?

Our sixth theme follows the other war that was taking place alongside the actual fighting: the war to gain recognition as a country. This theme explores colonial attempts to obtain needed foreign assistance. Recognition and aid from a major power such as France would make the difference between victory and defeat.

Our seventh theme allows the people of the past to show us some of the horrors of war—the primitive medical care of the time, the deaths in battle, the nightmare of prison ships. We explore the sometimes visceral hatred many British soldiers felt toward the Patriots, whom they considered to be traitors. Here we see a glimpse of what it would take to win the peace when the war is over.

The final theme is about winning and losing—the price of victory and defeat. We see the moment of triumph—the recognition that the Patriots had achieved the impossible. We look also at the face of defeat for the British with General Cornwallis's surrender at Yorktown. We end with a picture of the future, as the first ambassador to Great Britain from the United States meets his former king. We are able to do all this through the people who actually lived at the time. We will let them tell the story of this most amazing revolution.

The colonists complained that they had no voice in Britain's Parliament. Here members of the House of Commons meet in London.

Chapter I

The Road to Independence—The British and Loyalists Speak

THE AMERICAN REVOLUTION was fought over a misunderstanding about money. The British government had just finished fighting the French in the Seven Years War, called the French and Indian War in the colonies. It had been an expensive war, and Parliament needed to raise additional funds. It was decided that because the colonies had benefited from the war and had been protected by their mother country, it was only right that the colonists participate in raising revenue to pay for their own protection. The idea itself was not a bad one. The problem was that no one bothered to consult the colonists about it.

The colonists reacted to the new taxes and duties with anger. They were angry at having to pay additional fees to the British government. They felt that they had already paid for the French and Indian War by their own participation as soldiers fighting with the British army and through the hardships they had suffered from Indian raids. But more than their anger at the taxes themselves was their anger at how they had been levied. No one had consulted them. No one had treated them as full British citizens were supposed to be treated. This brought to mind a recurring issue for the colonists: the British government treated them as inferior citizens. Their voice was not heard in making policy that affected them. And thus was born the rallying cry of independence: "No taxation without representation."

At first the response in the colonies was unanimous. Colonial legislatures passed resolutions listing their grievances. They expected that their reminders to the king and Parliament would result in a response to their concerns. As the Virginia House of Burgesses pointed out, the colonists were asking only for "the privileges . . . possessed by the people of Great Britain." Parliament dealt with their requests in an unexpected way, which would eventually lead to war. Parliament told them, in effect, that they indeed did *not* have the same rights as other citizens of Britain.

This response resulted in intense discussions among the colonists about the best way to deal with Parliament's actions. Articles debating the issue began to appear in the newspapers. Groups formed to discuss ways of obtaining their rights. The discussion became more and more angry as time passed and Parliament increased its demands on the colonies. There were protests, some of which led to violence, as in the Boston Massacre. Within the colonies, the discussion began to divide the people. There were the Loyalists, who supported a peaceful negotiation of their grievances. They feared the response of the British government if their demands became too strident. They also felt that no one had a right to oppose the king. The other group became known as the Patriots.

Over time their demands for their rights would lead to discussion of the ultimate demand—separation from the mother country and the establishment of their own nation. In this chapter we will hear the voices of those nearly forgotten in history, the Loyalists and the British themselves.

Parliament Stirs Outrage in the Colonies: The Stamp Act

The Stamp Act, passed by the British Parliament and signed by King George III in March 1765, was the match that lit the fire of the Revolutionary War. Just about any official document that

The Stamp Act taxed many everyday items used by the colonists, from legal papers and deeds to newspapers and playing cards.

colonists would need in everyday life—a deed for a house, a will to pass on an estate to one's children, a license to practice business—would now require a special stamp to make it official, a stamp that colonists would have to pay for. They also would have to pay for a stamp to advertise in local newspapers. Even the playing cards one might buy would have to be stamped. Parliament may have seen the Stamp Act as simply a way to generate needed monies. The colonists saw it as taxation without representation.

WHEREAS BY AN ACT MADE in the last session of parliament, several duties were granted, continued, and appropriated, towards defraying the expenses of defending, protecting, and securing, the British colonies and plantations in America: and whereas it is just and necessary, that provision be made for raising a further revenue within your Majesty's dominions in America, towards defraying the said expences: we, your Majesty's most dutiful and loyal subjects, the commons of Great Britain, in parliament assembled, have therefore resolved to give and grant unto your Majesty the several rates and duties. . . . For every skin or piece of vellum or parchment, or sheet or piece of paper, on which shall be ingrossed, written or printed, any declaration, plea . . . in any court of law . . . a stamp duty of three pence . . . any petition . . . any will . . . certificate of any degree taken in any university . . . any licence, appointment, or admission of any . . . attorney . . . to practise in any court . . . any licence for the retailing of wine . . . any deed . . . by which any quantity of land . . . shall be granted, conveyed, or assigned . . . every

"It is just and necessary, that provision be made for raising a further revenue within your Majesty's dominions in America."

pack of playing cards, and all dice, which shall be sold or used within the said colonies . . . every pamphlet . . . every almanack or calendar . . . every advertisement to be contained in any gazette, news paper or other paper.

—*From Edmund S. Morgan, editor,* Prologue to Revolution: Sources and Documents on the Stamp Act Crisis, 1764–1766. *Chapel Hill, NC: University of North Carolina Press, 1959, pp. 35–41.*

Think about This

1. Why were the colonists upset when they learned about the Stamp Act?
2. Do you think the members of Parliament expected the colonists to protest against the new taxes?

A British Soldier Defends Himself

In 1770 the discussion among the colonists in Boston led to an event later known as the Boston Massacre. No one really knows what happened on the night of March 5 or why the British soldiers began firing into the crowd of protesting colonists. The officer in charge, Captain Thomas Preston, had to defend himself in court after he was accused of ordering the soldiers to fire their weapons. In the following deposition, he claims to have never given the order. Many Patriots claimed he had. Some Loyalists claimed that one of the Patriots in the crowd had shouted out the order. These Loyalists felt the Patriots were trying to create a reason for rebellion. Whoever started it, when the soldiers fired into the crowd of protestors, three were killed and eight others wounded, two of

The Boston Massacre united many of the colonists in their belief that the British would never treat them fairly.

whom later died. Patriots called it a massacre, and accounts of the event quickly spread throughout the colonies. The result was more bitterness toward the British and more support for the view that the British would never meet the colonists' reasonable demands.

Captain Preston told the court:

THE MOB STILL INCREASED and were more outrageous, striking their clubs or bludgeons one against another, and calling out, come on you rascals, you bloody backs, you lobster scoundrels, fire if you dare . . . fire and be damned, we know you dare not, and much more such language was used. At this time I was between the soldiers and the mob, parleying with, and endeavoring all in my power to persuade them to retire peaceably, but to no purpose. They advanced to the points of the bayonets, struck some of them and even the muzzles of the pieces, and seemed to be endeavoring to close with the soldiers. On which some well behaved persons asked me if the guns were charged. I replied yes. They then asked me if I intended to order the men to fire. I answered no, by no means, observing to them that I was advanced before the muzzles of the men's pieces, and must fall a sacrifice if they fired; that the soldiers were upon the half cocks and charged bayonets, and my giving the word fire under those circumstances would prove me to be no officer. While I was thus speaking, one of the soldiers having received a severe blow with a stick, stepped a little to one side and instantly fired.

"They then asked me if I intended to order the men to fire. I answered no, by no means."

—*From* Publications of the Colonial Society of Massachusetts, Vol. VII. *Boston: The Colonial Society of Massachusetts, 1905, pp. 8–9.*

Think about This

1. What in this testimony might lead you to think that Preston did not give the order to fire?
2. If you were a British soldier, how do you think you would have reacted to the protesters?

A Loyalist Preacher Is Silenced

The colonists who remained strong supporters of the king were known as Tories, Royalists, or (most often) Loyalists. They agreed with the other colonists that changes needed to be made, and that the Mother Country, Great Britain, should agree to the just demands of the colonists. But they felt strongly that the solution lay in negotiation and discussion with Great Britain. As the Patriots became more ardent and moved closer toward a position of demanding independence, they began to harass the Loyalists, pressuring them to support the cause. Jonathan Boucher, a Loyalist minister in Annapolis, Maryland, later wrote in his memoir about his experiences as a community leader who resisted the increasing call for revolution.

mischiefs *in this sense, the early acts of rebellion against Britain*

OTHER TROUBLES ALSO soon came upon us. The times grew dreadfully uneasy, and I was neither an unconcerned nor an idle spectator of the mischiefs that were gathering. . . . Though I really had no views nor wishes but such as I believed to be for the true interest of the country, all the forward and noisy patriots, both in the Assembly and out of it, agreed to consider me as an obnoxious person. . . . I endeavoured in my sermons, and in various pieces published in the Gazettes of the country, to check the immense mischief that was impending, but I endeavoured in vain. I was soon restrained from preaching, and the Press was no longer open to me. The first open and avowed violence I met with was on account of my expressly declining . . . to preach a sermon to recommend the suffering people of Boston to the charity of my parish. Their port was shut up by Act of Parliament; and as it was alleged that they suffered thus in the common cause, contributions were collected for them all over the continent: the true motive was by these means to raise a sum sufficient to purchase arms and ammunition. I also refused to set my hand to various Associations and Resolves, all, in my estimation, very unnecessary, unwise, and unjust. In consequence of which I soon became a marked man; and though I endeavoured to conduct myself with all possible temper and even caution, I daily met with insults, indignities, and injuries.

"I daily met with insults, indignities, and injuries."

—*From Jonathan Boucher,* Reminiscences of an American Loyalist. *Boston: Houghton Mifflin Company, 1925, pp. 92–93, 104–105.*

Think about This

1. What did Boucher decline to do in regard to the people of Boston that made him a "marked" man?
2. Did the Loyalists have a right to express their views before war broke out? Did they still have this right after the war began?
3. Did the Patriots have a right to harass those who remained loyal to the king?

An Angry Loyalist Speaks Out against the Patriots' Scare Tactics

Many Loyalists had serious complaints about the actions of those who wanted independence. One such person was a Massachusetts

As war approached, those who still supported King George III, the Loyalists, sometimes suffered at the hands of the Patriots, who wanted to be free of his rule.

resident, writing under the name "Plain English," who spoke out in an article for a Loyalist newspaper. He detailed specific cases of Loyalists threatened and abused by their neighbors for refusing to support the Patriot cause. Written just a month before the war began, the article shows just how divided the colonists were.

TO REPRESENT TO YOU the distresses of some of those people, who, from a sense of their duty to the king, and a reverence for his laws, have behaved quietly and peaceably; and for which reason they have been deprived of their liberty, abused in their persons, and suffered such barbarous cruelties, insults, and indignities, besides the loss of their property, by the hands of lawless mobs and riots, as would have been disgraceful even for savages to have committed. The courts of justice being shut up in most parts of the province, and the justices of those courts compelled by armed force . . . to refrain from doing their duties, at present it is rendered impracticable for those sufferers to obtain redress. . . . Daniel Leonard was driven from his house, and bullets fired into it by the mob, and he obliged to take refuge in Boston, for the supposed crime of obeying his Majesty's requisition. . . . Brigadier Ruggles was also attacked by another party, who were routed after having painted and cut the hair off of one of his horse's mane and tail. . . . [Mr. Sewall's] house at Cambridge was attacked by a mob, and his windows were broken. . . . In August, Colonel Putnam of Worcester, a firm friend to Government, had two fat cows stolen and taken from him, and a very valuable grist-mill burnt. . . . Thomas Foster, Esq., an ancient gentleman, was obliged to run into the woods, and had like to have been lost, and the mob, although the justices, with Mr. Foster, were sitting in the town, ransacked his house, and damaged his furniture. . . . Jesse Dunbar, of Halifax, in Plymouth county, bought some fat cattle of Mr. Thomas . . . finding he bought it of Mr. Thomas, they put the ox into a cart, and fixing Dunbar in his belly, carted him four miles, and there made him pay a dollar, after taking three more cattle and a horse from him. The Plymouth mob delivered him to the Kingston mob, which

"Daniel Leonard was driven from his house, and bullets fired into it by the mob . . . for the supposed crime of obeying his Majesty's requisition."

carted him four miles further, and forced from him another dollar, then delivered him to the Duxborough mob, who abused him by throwing the tripe in his face, and endeavoring to cover him with it to the endangering his life. . . .

To recount the suffering of all from mobs, rioters, and trespassers, would take more time and paper than can be spared for that purpose. It is hoped the foregoing will be sufficient to put you upon the use of proper means and measures for giving relief to all that have been injured by such unlawful and wicked practices.

—From Rivington's Gazette, *March 9, 1775. In Frank Moore,* Diary of the American Revolution from Newspapers and Original Documents, Vol. I. *New York: Charles Scribner, 1860, pp. 37–42.*

Think about This

1. What do you think "Plain English" meant by the term *mob*?
2. Why were the Loyalists mentioned here unable to "obtain redress"?
3. Would the actions taken against the Loyalists have been justified if the war had already begun?

A Newspaper Announces British Plans

In April 1775 someone from London sent information to a colonial newspaper about new orders that had been given to the British troops in Boston. When the newspaper printed the following report, the Patriots knew that the moment of confrontation would soon come to pass.

A ROYAL PROCLAMATION, declaring the inhabitants of Massachusetts Bay, and some others in the different colonies, actual rebels, with a blank commission to try and execute such of them as he can get hold of. With this is sent a list of names to be inserted in the commission, as he may judge expedient. Messrs. Samuel Adams, John Adams, Robert Treat Paine, and John Hancock, of Massachusetts Bay; John Dickinson, of Philadelphia; Peyton Randolph, of Virginia; and Henry Middleton, of South Carolina, are particularly named, with several others. This black list the General will no doubt keep to himself, and unfold it gradually as he finds it convenient. Every mark of power is preparing to be shown to the Americans. Three general officers are appointed to go with the next troops. They are Generals Burgoyne, Clinton, and Howe. A considerable number of men are drafted from the three regiments of guards, and ordered to hold themselves in readiness to embark for America immediately. Four regiments from Ireland, one of them light dragoons, are under sailing orders for Boston, with several capital ships of war, and six cutters, to obstruct the American trade, and prevent all Europeans goods from going there, particularly arms and ammunition.—Oh, poor America!

blank commission *a document giving the British officers permission to arrest any Patriot leader even if they did not know for certain that he had committed a crime*

—From Holt's Journal, *April 13, 1775. In Frank Moore,* Diary of the American Revolution from Newspapers and Original Documents, Vol. I. *New York: Charles Scribner, 1860, pp. 60–61.*

Think about This

1. With more than two hundred years of hindsight, it is hard to imagine that Patriot names like John Adams, Robert Paine, and John Hancock were ever on a "black list," liable to be arrested and shot. It gives us a sense of the real dangers these American heroes faced. It also gives us pause for thought: what if the Revolutionary War had been lost? Would Adams and the others be remembered as heroes today, or merely disloyal rebels?
2. What did the phrase "every mark of power" mean in the British report?

In a rousing speech in the Virginia House of Burgesses, orator Patrick Henry was one of the first to voice his opposition to the Stamp Act.

Chapter 2

The Road to Independence—The Colonists Speak

THE STAMP ACT, as we have seen, was passed by Parliament in 1765. The first battle of the Revolutionary War did not occur until April 19, 1775. During the years of discussion, more was happening in the colonies than just division among the colonists themselves. As the road to independence neared, the colonists began to form the lawmaking bodies that would be the foundation of the new nation.

The Committees of Correspondence were formed in individual communities in 1772, mainly to coordinate information and responses to Great Britain. Out of them grew the First Continental Congress, which met in Philadelphia from September to October of 1774. The first legislative body of the soon-to-be new nation sent a petition to King George III, known as the Declaration of Rights and Grievances.

As war neared various colonies created "shadow" governments, such as the Provincial Congress of the Massachusetts Bay Colony. These would become the basis of state governments as the Revolution progressed.

The actual outbreak of war with the attacks on Lexington and Concord, Massachusetts, in April 1775 showed the need for a national body to govern the colonies and conduct the war. Each colony sent representatives to Pennsylvania once again, and the Second Continental Congress convened on May 10, 1775. One of its first actions was to appoint a commander in chief—George Washington—for the as yet nonexistent Continental Army. Another early action was to send what came to be known as the Olive Branch Petition to King George III in July 1775.

The king and Parliament rejected this last chance for peace. Both sides continued to mobilize for war. The Second Continental Congress, usually called simply the Continental Congress, discussed the possible contents of a document that would sever the colonies from the mother country.

On July 2, 1776, that document—the Declaration of Independence—was passed by the Continental Congress, and with its proclamation on July 4, a new nation came into being.

Initially, however, the colonial protests were polite and measured. Reading the documents today, you get the sense that the colonists expected Parliament would be reasonable and reconsider its actions.

"Illegal, Unconstitutional, and Unjust": Virginia's House of Burgesses Confronts King George

Virginia's House of Burgesses was one of the first colonial legislatures to respond to the Stamp Act. Its members were not advocating revolution, however. They were simply asking for the "ancient" privileges that they had long enjoyed as British citizens. This excerpt is from a resolution the House of Burgesses passed in May 1765.

> RESOLVED, That the first adventurers and settlers of this his Majesty's colony and dominion of Virginia, brought with them, and transmitted to their posterity . . . all the privileges and immunities that have at any time been held, enjoyed, and possessed by the people of Great Britain. . . . Resolved, That his Majesty's liege people of this his most ancient colony, have enjoyed the right of being thus governed by their own assembly, in the article of taxes and internal police [policies] . . . Resolved, Therefore, that the General Assembly of this colony . . . have, in their representative capacity, the only exclusive right and power to lay taxes and impositions upon the inhabitants of this colony; and that every attempt to vest such a power in any person or persons whatsoever, other than the General Assembly aforesaid, is illegal, unconstitutional, and unjust, and has a manifest tendency to destroy British, as well as American freedom.

"Resolved . . . that the General Assembly of this colony . . . have . . . the only exclusive right and power to lay taxes."

—*From* A Collection of Interesting, Authentic Papers, Relative to the Dispute between Great Britain and America. *London: J. Almon, 1777, p. 7.*

Think about This

1. What reasons do the colonists give for saying that they are the only ones who can levy taxes?
2. How could levying taxes "destroy British, as well as American freedom"?

Massachusetts Prepares to Fight

Massachusetts Patriots were the most vocal supporters of independence as the crisis continued over the years. Their "shadow" government, the Provincial Congress, was among the first to prepare for battle.

February 20.—The Provincial Congress of Massachusetts Bay has resolved: that the great law of self-preservation calls upon the inhabitants of that colony, immediately to prepare against every attempt that may be made to attack them by surprise. And, upon serious deliberation, most earnestly recommended to the militia in general, as well as the detached part of it in minute-men, that they spare neither time, pains, nor expenses, at so critical a juncture, in perfecting themselves forthwith in military discipline; and that skilful instructors be provided for those companies which are not already provided therewith. It also recommends to the towns and districts in that colony, that they encourage such persons as are skilled in the manufactory of fire-arms and bayonets, diligently to apply themselves there for supplying such of the inhabitants as shall be deficient.

—*From* Gaines Mercury, *February 27, 1775. In Frank Moore,* Diary of the American Revolution from Newspapers and Original Documents, Vol. I. *New York: Charles Scribner, 1860, p. 25.*

Think about This

1. The Provincial Congress was not the official legislature of the colony. Did it have the right to order the militia to prepare?
2. Would the British government think the colonists meant to attack the soldiers, or only to defend themselves?

The Continental Congress Names a Military Leader

The attack did indeed come, in April 1775. The Continental Congress, meeting in Philadelphia, responded to the battles of Lexington and Concord in Massachusetts by appointing a Virginia planter, George Washington, as commander in chief of the Continental Army. In the 1750s Washington had fought shoulder to shoulder with British troops in the French and Indian War. He became a hero, leading the Virginia militia and gaining the respect of British and Americans alike. Now, some twenty years later, the British would be his enemy. John Hancock, president of the Continental Congress, recorded the instructions given to Washington on his appointment.

> THIS CONGRESS having Appointed you to be General and Commander in Chief of the Army of the United Colonies and of all the Forces Raised or to be Raised by them, and of all others who shall voluntarily offer their Service and Join the said Army for the Defence of American Liberty, and for Repelling every hostile invasion thereof; You are to Repair with all Expedition to the Colony of Massachusetts Bay, & Take Charge of the Army of the United Colonies. . . . You are to Victual [feed] at the Continental Expense all such Volunteers as have Joined or shall Join the United Army. . . . You shall take every Method in your power consistent with Providence to Destroy or make Prisoners all Persons who now are, or who hereafter shall appear in Arms against the good people of the United Colonies . . . And whereas all particulars cannot be foreseen, nor positive instructions for such Emergencies so before hand given . . . You are therefore upon all such Accidents or any Occasions that may happen to use

John Hancock was president of the Continental Congress at the time that George Washington was appointed commander in chief of the Continental Army.

your best Circumspection and Advising with your Council of War to Order and Dispose of the said Army under your Command as may be most Advantageous for the Obtaining the End for which these forces have been Raised, making it your special care in Discharge of the great trust Committed unto you, that the Liberties of America Receive no Detriment.

—*From Record Book No. 2, "Letters and Doings of Congress—from 17 June 1775 to 16 March 1776,"* Papers of John Hancock. *Manuscript Division, Library of Congress.*

Think about This

1. What important concern did the instructions to Washington contain regarding American liberties? Whose liberties were the representatives concerned about?
2. What specific orders were given in these instructions?
3. The colonies have not yet declared their independence. Explain why you think the Continental Congress was right or wrong in forming an army at this time.

Washington Writes Home

The risk taken by those who led the opposition to Great Britain was very real. Each of the members of the Continental Congress, each of the officers appointed to the Continental Army, knew that he would be tried and executed for treason if the colonies did not win the war. George Washington, accepting the position of commander in chief of the new Continental Army, wrote home to his wife, Martha, on June 18, 1775, explaining why he felt he must take on this risk.

My Dearest

I am now set down to write to you on a subject which fills me with inexpressible concern—and this concern is greatly aggravated and Increased when I reflect on the uneasiness I know it will give you.—It has been determined in Congress that the whole army raised for the defence of the American Cause shall be put under my care, and that it is necessary for me to proceed immediately to Boston to take upon me the Command of it.—You may believe me my dear Patcy [Martha's nickname], when I assure you, in the most solemn manner, that so far from seeking this appointment I have used every endeavor in my power to avoid it, not only from my unwillingness to part with you and the Family, but from a consciousness of its being a trust too great for my Capacity, and that I should enjoy more real happiness and felicity in one month with you at home, than I have the most distant prospect of reaping abroad, if my stay was to be seven times seven years.—But, as it has been a kind of destiny that has thrown me upon this Service, I shall hope that my undertaking of it, is designed to answer some good purpose—You might and I suppose did perceive, from the Tenor of my letters, that I was apprehensive I could not avoid this appointment, as I did not even pretend to intimate when I should return—that was the case—it was utterly out of my power to refuse this appointment without exposing my Character to such censure as would have reflected dishonour upon myself, and given pain to my friends—this I am sure could not, and ought not to be pleasing to you, and must have lessened me considerably in my own esteem.—I shall rely therefore, confidently, on that Providence which has heretofore preserved, and been bountiful to me, not doubting but

"... so far from seeking this appointment I have used every endeavor in my power to avoid it."

that I shall return safe to you in the fall.—I shall feel no pain from the Toil, or the danger of the campaign—My unhappiness will flow, from the uneasiness I know you will feel at being left alone & I therefore beg of you to summon your whole fortitude and Resolution and pass your time as agreeably as possible.

—From letter of George Washington to Martha Washington, Philadelphia, June 18, 1775, a copy made from the original in 1849 and contained in the Henley Smith Collection. *Manuscript Division, Library of Congress.*

Think about This

1. What were Washington's reasons for accepting the appointment?
2. Why would he have liked to decline it?
3. Does Washington show courage in this letter? How?

The Colonies Declare Their Independence

Although the Revolutionary War began in April 1775, it was not until July 4, 1776, that the colonies actually declared independence from Great Britain. The text of the Declaration of Independence was written primarily by a Virginian, Thomas Jefferson, who would later serve as the third president of the United States. A portion of his eloquent words follows.

WE HOLD THESE TRUTHS to be self-evident, that all men are created equal, that they are endowed by their Creator with certain unalienable Rights, that among these are Life, Liberty and the pursuit of Happiness. That to secure these rights, Governments are instituted among

A draft of the Declaration of Independence in Jefferson's own handwriting

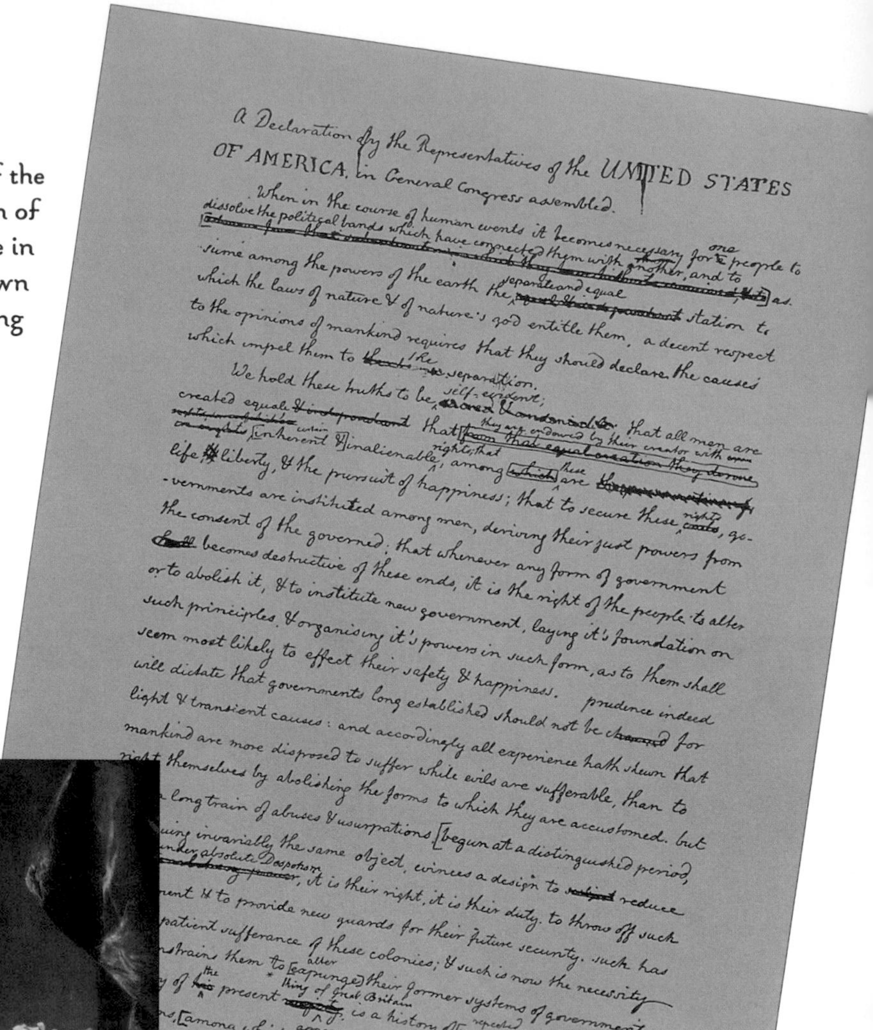

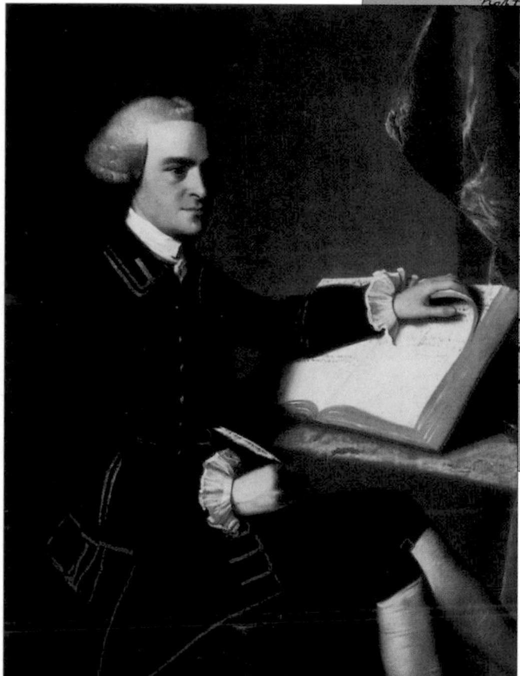

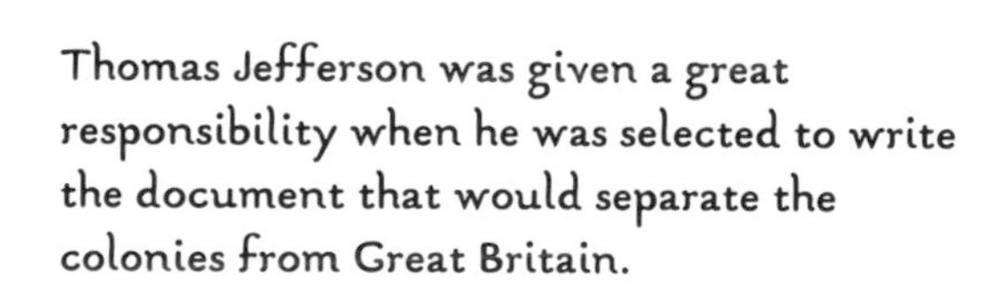

Thomas Jefferson was given a great responsibility when he was selected to write the document that would separate the colonies from Great Britain.

Men, deriving their just powers from the consent of the governed. That whenever any Form of Government becomes destructive of these ends, it is the Right of the People to alter or to abolish it. . . .

> *"We hold these truths to be self-evident . . ."*

We, therefore, the Representatives of the united States of America, in General Congress, Assembled, appealing to the Supreme Judge of the world for the rectitude of our intentions, do, in the Name, and by Authority of the good People of these Colonies, solemnly publish and declare, That these United Colonies are, and of Right ought to be Free and Independent States; that they are Absolved from all Allegiance to the British Crown, and that all political connection between them and the State of Great Britain, is and ought to be totally dissolved; and that as Free and Independent States, they have full Power to levy War, conclude Peace, contract Alliances, establish Commerce, and to do all other Acts and Things which Independent States may of right do. And for the support of this Declaration, with a firm reliance on the protection of divine Providence, we mutually pledge to each other our Lives, our Fortunes and our sacred Honor.

Think about This

1. Why did Jefferson and other members of the Continental Congress believe the colonies had the right to rebel?
2. If you were King George III, how would you have defended your position?

The American Revolutionary War soldier did not have the neat military appearance of his opponents in battle.

Chapter 3

To Be a Soldier

THE ARMIES THAT FACED EACH OTHER during the Revolutionary War could not have been more different. The British soldiers were considered the best in the world. They were well supplied, well trained, and well disciplined. In their distinctive red uniforms (which earned them the nicknames "Redcoats," "Bloody Backs," and "Lobsterbacks"), they marched into battle in straight lines that never seemed to falter. The British government would send 50,000 of these troops to the colonies during the course of the war. The British would also pay for the services of an additional 30,000 German mercenaries, the dreaded Hessians. Many of the Loyalists living in the colonies would also fight with the British troops. The number of Loyalist soldiers is estimated to have been at least 8,000.

The Patriots were homegrown soldiers. Some of them did have a little military experience. These colonists, formed into local militias, had fought with the British against the French in the French and Indian War. They had learned something of British tactics and had gained some understanding of the life of the soldier. However, this knowledge often seemed to make the task of fighting the British more difficult. They knew enough to know what kind of soldier they faced. And they knew that they lacked the skills needed to effectively fight that kind of soldier.

Creating soldiers from the untrained colonists would not be an easy task. The problem was made more difficult by a lack of supplies, such as uniforms and equipment. General Washington spent a great deal of time—time that would have been better spent on training—trying to get the Continental Congress to authorize the money to pay for supplies. Despite all these problems, Washington's Continentals held on against the British until 1778, when foreign help enhanced their prospects for achieving victory. Prussian Baron von Steuben arrived that year and trained the American soldiers in military tactics. Several thousand French troops also arrived, adding disciplined fighting power to the army. Other foreign countries provided money for supplies.

It is important to remember, however, that Washington had managed to hold the British and Hessians in check from April 1775 until the spring of 1778. The Americans had learned to be soldiers on their own, managing to win such crucial battles as Saratoga in October 1777 before their foreign allies arrived on the scene. The process of becoming soldiers was not easy, but determination, discipline, and Washington's persistent nagging for supplies got the job done.

An Official Notice Encourages Men to Volunteer

Military units during the Revolutionary War kept "Orderly Books," which included all the official letters, orders, and communications

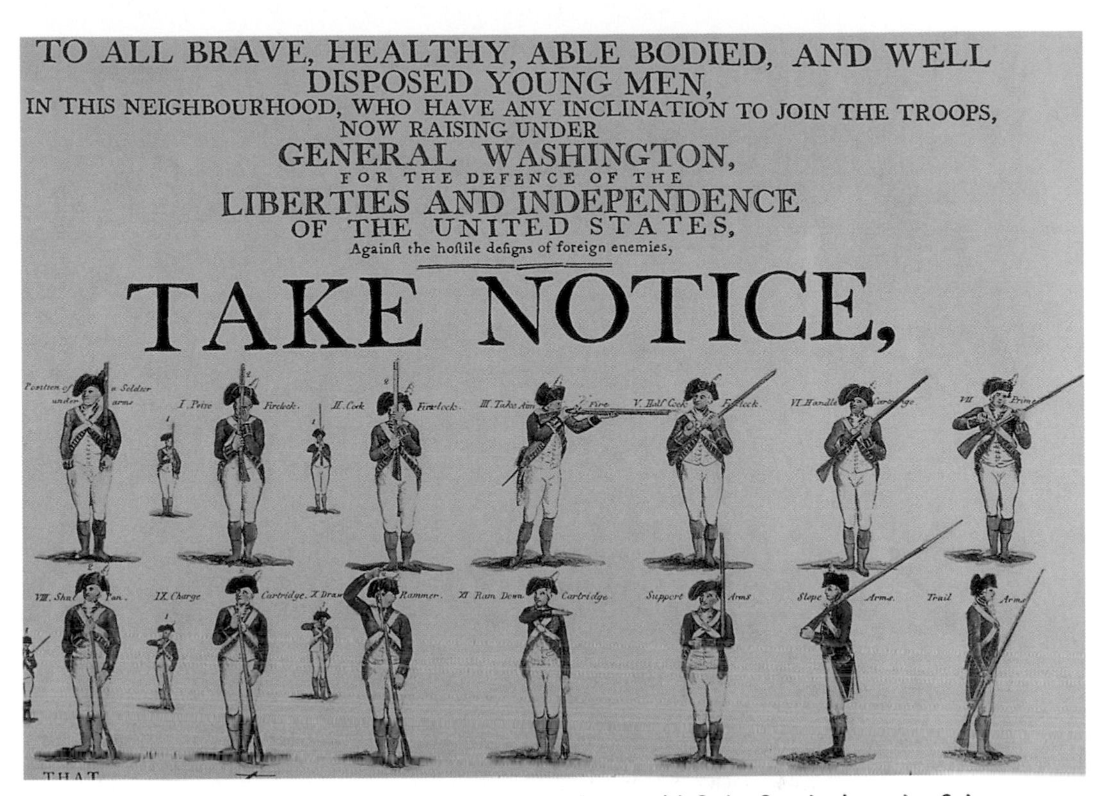

The Continental Army needed to recruit men who would fight for the length of the war and offered them incentives to join through posters like this one.

among the officers. From the Fort Ticonderoga Orderly Book comes this description of the benefits to be offered to those who served in the fight for independence. In actual fact, those who came did so more because they believed in the cause than for any "gratuities" they might gain. Among those who supported the Revolution, there was much devotion and willingness to sacrifice—especially among New Englanders.

THE CONGRESS OF THE UNITED STATES have for the Reward and Encouragement of every Non Commission'd Officer and Soldier who shall engage to serve during the War further resolve to give (over

". . . no American will hesitate to enroll himself to defend his Country and Posterity from every Attempt of Tyranny to enslave it."

and above the Bounty of Twenty Dollars) to each Man Annually one Complete Suit of Cloathing which for the Present Year is to consist of Two Linnen Hunting Shirts, Two Pear of Stockings, Two Pear of Shoes, Two Pear of Over Alls, a Leathren or Woolen Jackett with Sleeves, One Pear of Breeches and One Leather Cap or Hatt, amounting in the Whole to the Value of 20 Dollars or that Sum to be paid to each Soldier who shall procure these Articles for himself & Produce a Certificate thereof from the Captn of the Company to which he belongs to the Pay-Master of the Regt. This Noble Bounty of 20 Dollars & One Hundered Acres of Land at the End of the War is such an Ample and Generous Gratuity from the United States, that the Genl is convins'd [convinced] no American will hesitate to enroll himself to defend his Country and Posterity from every Attempt of Tyranny to enslave it.

—*From* Orderly Book of the Northern Army at Ticonderoga and Mt. Independence, from October 17th, 1776 to January 8th, 1777. *Albany, NY: J. Munsell, 1859, pp. 24–25.*

Think about This

1. What benefits would a soldier receive for enlisting?
2. Do you think the Congress was offering enough to make it worthwhile to enlist?

Disciplining the Soldiers: The Record of a Court-Martial

Although the Continental Army was filled with highly motivated men—soldiers defending not only their liberties but also their homeland—it suffered from the same discipline problems that plagued most armies. Especially as conditions worsened and victory seemed impossible, desertion was a problem. One issue was that the soldiers could not accept the requirement that they remain with the army during the nonfighting season. Many returned home to take care of their families and came back when they were able. The soldiers did not see this as desertion, but their officers did. At the same time, there were the usual camp problems brought on by boredom—drinking, gambling, and fighting. The Orderly Books show a steady record of court-martial trials to deal with the problems. The penalties may seem harsh to us, but they were a normal part of eighteenth-century military discipline.

AT A GEN'L COURT MARTIAL whereof Colo. Courtland was President Feb. 7th, Thomas Scott in the 3rd Pennl Regimt Tryed for Deserting to the Enemy and Unanamously acquited. Thoms Lawler of the 4th Pennl Regt also Tryed for the same Crime found Guilty and Sintance to Recieve one Hundred lashes on his beare Back well Laid on also John Henry of the 7th Virginia Regt Tryed for the Same Crime and acquited Likewise Thomas Whitney of Capt. Bowdens Compy of artillery Tryed for the Same Crime found Guilty and Sintance to Recieve One Hundred Lashes on his beare Back Well Laid on. At the Same Court Marl William Marvis of the 9th Pennl Regt Tryed for geting Drunk Threatning the Life of one Cameron and Hutchings and kicking Hutchings Down and also for Stricking the Corporal of the Quatr. Guard when confined and Denis Henly of the Same Regt. tryed for abusing The Said Cameron and Threatning to desert as soon as he had got his Shoes and cursing Congress William Marvis found guilty of Stricking the Corpl of the Qur Guard When under Confinement. That being a Breach of the 6th article and 18th Section of the articles of Warr the Court Sintince him to

The winter of 1777–1778 was a terrible one for the soldiers camping at Valley Forge and may have contributed to some of the offenses the men committed.

Receive thirty Lashes on his beare Barck well Laid on—The Commander in Chief approves of all Those Sintances against Lawler Low Whitney Marvis and Kinsley and order The Punishment to be Executed to Morrow Morning at Roll Call at the Heads of the Respective Regiments to which they belong. Scott to be Emediately Released from his Confinement and also Henry who are to join their Regiments.

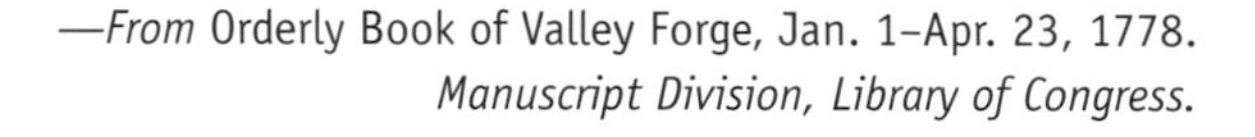

—*From* Orderly Book of Valley Forge, Jan. 1–Apr. 23, 1778.
Manuscript Division, Library of Congress.

Think about This

1. What kinds of crimes were these soldiers tried for, and what punishments went with each crime?
2. Why do you think the army needed to use this kind of discipline?

Washington's Letter to John Hancock: Send Money

The problem of getting needed supplies seemed to be a constant one for General Washington and his staff. In today's military, there are whole groups of people whose job it is to see that the soldiers are supplied. But the burden of supplying the Continental Army fell mainly on Washington himself. Adding to the problem was the fact that each colony had to be petitioned separately, and some were better than others at providing their fair share. Problems with the value of the Continental money also caused confusion and difficulties. This letter to John Hancock, president of the Continental Congress, illustrates the problems Washington encountered.

CAMP AT CAMBRIDGE, SEPT 7TH 1775

Sir,

I do myself the Honour of addressing you in Consequence of an application from the Commissary General, who is by my Direction, taking all proper Precaution on the approach of Winter. I desired him to commit to Writing such Proposals as his Experience and Knowledge of the Country, might entitle him to make, which he has done in the Paper I have the Honour to enclose. The Difficulty of procuring a sufficient Quantity of Salt, which I objected to him, he has fully obviated, by assuring me that there is so much now actually in Store in this and the neighboring Towns, as will remove all Possibility of a Disappointment.

"I . . . request that more Money may be forwarded with all Expedition, the military Chest being nearly exhausted."

A soldier of the Continental Army carried this wallet, which contains currency printed by New Jersey. There was as yet no national currency.

I propose to do myself the Honour of writing in a few days fully and particularly on several Heads, to which I must now refer. In the Mean Time I have only to inform the Congress that I have received a small Supply of 7000 lbs of Powder this Week from Rhode Island, and in a few Days expect 7 Tons of Lead and 500 Hand of Arms, being a Part of the same Importation; and to request that more Money may be forwarded with all Expedition, the military Chest being nearly exhausted.

I am with the greatest Respect Sir, your most obed. & very hble servt

G.o Washington

—From letter of George Washington to John Hancock, Sept. 7, 1775, contained in Record Book No. 2, "Letters and Doings of Congress—from 17 June 1775 to 16 March 1776," Papers of John Hancock. *Manuscript Division, Library of Congress.*

Think about This

1. What items was General Washington most concerned about in this particular letter?
2. Why do you think Washington was so concerned about the provisions of salt?

An Officer's Appeal: Bad Food Makes for Unhappy Men

At the lower levels of command, the officers were equally frustrated with the scarcity of provisions. This letter between two brothers, both serving in the Continental Army, captures the frustration and anger of those in the field trying to make do without enough to eat.

WE HAVE BEEN WITHOUT bread or Rice more than five days out of seven, for these three Weeks past—and the Prospect remains as fair as it hath been. . . . The Provision we draw hath been Chiefly Salt Beef, and that alone without bread or Potatoes is tedious—It appears to me that unless the Army is better Supplied, you had better disband them now, rather than fill the Regiment. . . . If the Fault lies at the door of any Individual, deliver him to us for a sacrifice, as it would be more acceptable to us, if we must be starved, first to imbrue our hands in the Blood of him who brought us to it. . . . This whole part of the Country are Starving for want of bread, they have been drove to the necessity of Grinding Flaxseed & oats together for bread—Is it not Possible for the State to do something else besides Promises, Promises cannot feed or Clothe a Man always—Performance is sometime necessary to make a man believe you intend to Preform [perform].

"It appears to me that unless the Army is better Supplied, you had better disband them now."

—*From Ebenezer Huntington,* Letters Written by Ebenezer Huntington during the American Revolution. *New York: Chas. Fred. Heartman, 1914, pp. 80–81.*

Think about This

1. If you were the officer, how would you tell your troops that supplies were short?
2. What do you think it does to soldiers' morale if their food does not come regularly?

Chapter 4

On the Battlefield

THROUGHOUT HISTORY wars have been fought by certain "rules of engagement." At the time of the Revolutionary War, the rules had been relatively unchanged for seventeen hundred years, since the time of the Roman army. The only major changes were in the weapons. Revolutionary War soldiers used muskets that fired lead balls driven by gunpowder, replacing the bows and arrows, swords, and lances of medieval times. Cannons had replaced the old-fashioned battering rams and trebuchets of the past. Nevertheless, the soldiers still lined up facing each other across an open field, marched to within 50 yards of the enemy's line, fired off several rounds of ammunition, and then attacked each other with bayonets. That sort of formal fighting was disastrous for the members of the Continental Army. They did not have the superiority in numbers to hold the field in that kind of fight, nor were they well trained.

The Continental Army's success during the critical early years of the war came from a willingness to change the rules. The outnumbered Americans were most successful when they fought the

American soldiers drive off the British in the woods of Penobscot, Maine.

war their own way. They harassed the enemy soldiers, attacked as snipers from the woods, crossed the Delaware River in the middle of the night and attacked the Hessians at Trenton the day after Christmas, when they were sleeping off their celebrations of the previous day. These "ungentlemanly" tactics absolutely shocked the British and their allies.

The Americans succeeded also because they learned to use the land itself as a weapon. The colonies were densely forested and hilly. The heavily equipped British and Hessian troops often were stopped for days just trying to create roads through the rugged terrain. The dense terrain also contributed to solving the problem of the outnumbered Continental Army. The British and Hessians had to send in smaller numbers of soldiers at a time, giving the Americans a better chance at improving their odds in battle.

The number of soldiers who were actually involved in a battle would surprise us today. Some Revolutionary War "battles" would be considered just minor skirmishes today. The opening British attack on Lexington and Concord only involved 750 British soldiers. In their critical loss at Saratoga, the British and Hessian army fielded only about 6,500 men. In the final major battle of the war, at Yorktown, the British were outnumbered when the combined American and French armies of 16,000 soldiers defeated their 8,500. In comparison, the Allied landing on the beaches of Normandy in France during World War II involved 156,000 troops attacking the German positions. It's difficult to believe that such a small number of people were involved in the fighting that created an entire nation!

A Soldier Witnesses an Attack on General Washington

The Continental Army suffered terrible defeats and losses when General Washington took it into the field in 1776. Many times the only way that the army and its supplies made it to safety was a lucky decision by the British to approach from a different angle. The soldiers were devoted to General Washington, and one can imagine their relief when the incident described here left him unhurt.

AT EARLY DAWN we began to move toward the White plains, falling Trees into the Road and casting Stones and whatever might obstruct the Ordnance [cannons] of the Enemy the Party arrives at 9am—At 11 am the Enemy's Light Horse said to have been 800 strong hove in sight on a Ridge of Hills. . . . Had the Enemy continued to keep the main Road for One mile, they must have taken all the Provisions collected for the American Army, but by filing off to the left, a chance was left for us to get most of them to a safer place. At Noon the British Forces came up and formed on the Ridge when the Action was commenced and continued till Sun set—A remarkable instance of Providence happened to Gen'l Washington when riding on another Ridge N[orth] of the Brook a shot came from the Enemy & struck directly under his Horse's belly when in full gallop,—but did him no Injury—As soon as it was dark, Orders were given to retreat further into the Interiour, Every One carrying what he could—For a Week or two we lay undisturbed by the British—but soon retreated to Croton Heightc when Winter Quarters were intended.

—From the diary of William Jennison, Manuscript Division, Library of Congress.

Think about This

1. Why do you think a soldier would be so concerned about his general's safety?
2. Why were the soldiers given the job of cutting down trees and moving stones into the road?

Remembering Retreat and Imprisonment: An American's Journal

These diary entries are by a soldier involved in the unsuccessful attack on Montreal in May 1776. Soldiers fighting in the north feared not only the British and Canadian forces, but also their Native American allies.

[MAY 19TH] In the forenoon came the Kings Colors in View: our flag of truce met with them and after a long parley our officers surrendered up the Fort and now we are prisoners. The Lord protect us and keep us from harm. [May 20] In the afternoon, news came that a party of our men was coming for our relief. We that are prisoners were all ordered into the church and there shut up till the action was over. . . . Our men saw that they could retreat no further, surrendered up their arms to the Canadians, and themselves prisoners. The savages [Native Americans] were determined to cut off every man of them, but was prevented by the officers promising them our plunder. Accordingly the savages strip'd them almost naked and delivered them up to the Kings Troops. [May 26] Sunday at 2 oclock came [into] view 500 of our men commanded by Gen'l Arnold. . . . To our misfortune the savages discovered them and came in haste to drive us out

"Nothing but scenes of misery and woe attend us."

of sight of our army . . . drove the rest of us down the island as far as they could get us, through swamps and water as high as our waist. At last they came to a creek that was deep and swift. One man swam across, another set out but was unhappily drowned. This was the awfullest sight that ever my eyes beheld. Nothing but scenes of misery and woe attend us.

—From the journal of Benjamin Stevens, Manuscript Division, Library of Congress.

Think about This

1. Who do you think was giving the orders to the Native Americans?
2. What might have motivated Native Americans to help the British?
3. Why does Stevens use the term *savages*? Would such a term be acceptable today?

On the March to Escape the British Advance

This account comes from an officer who was part of Washington's retreat from a closely following British army late in 1776. Captain Anderson captures the sense of danger the soldiers must have felt as they tried to escape to safety.

THE BRITISH WERE NOW in chase of us with twenty thousand men, within three miles of us. We continued on our retreat;—our Regiment in the rear, and I, with thirty men, in rear of the Regiment, and General Washington in my rear with pioneers,—tearing up bridges and cutting down trees, to impede the march of the enemy. . . .

In the afternoon of the next day, we crossed the Delaware into

Pennsylvania, and in two hours afterwards the British appeared on the opposite bank and cannonaded us; but we were in the woods and bushes and none were wounded that I heard of.

This was the crisis of American danger. This night we lay amongst the leaves without tents or blankets, laying down with our feet to the fire. It was very cold. We had meat, but no bread. We had nothing to cook with, but our ramrods, which we run through a piece of meat and roasted it over the fire, and to hungry soldiers it tasted sweet.

"This night we lay amongst the leaves without tents or blankets, laying down with our feet to the fire."

The next day we moved up the Delaware. In this way we lived, crouching among the bushes, till about the twelfth of December.

—From Enoch Anderson, Personal Recollections of Captain Enoch Anderson. *Wilmington, DE: Historical Society of Delaware, 1896, p. 28.*

Think about This

1. Do you think this kind of experience makes better soldiers or weakens the army?
2. Do you think the British expected this kind of fight—a fleeing enemy laying down obstacles to slow their advance?

A British Soldier Complains: The Americans Are Not Fighting Fair

When the Continental Army began to adapt the rules of war to meet their best abilities, the British were shocked, as this soldier's account shows.

A British grenadier was a well-trained soldier, with a proper uniform and equipment to fight effectively.

DURING THE BATTLE the Americans were guilty of such a breach of all military rules as could not fail to exasperate our soldiers. The action was chiefly in the woods, interspersed with a few open fields. Two companies of grenadiers . . . observed a number of Americans . . . coming across the field with their arms clubbed, which is always considered to be a surrender . . . when the Americans had got within ten yards, they in an instant turned around their muskets, fired upon the grenadiers, and ran as fast as they could into the woods.

—From Thomas Anburey, With Burgoyne from Quebec. *Toronto: Macmillan of Canada, 1963, p. 141.*

Think about This

1. Why did the Americans have to use different tactics?
2. Do you think the British were right to feel that the only honorable way to fight was the way armies had traditionally fought?

One Hessian's Strong Feelings against the Americans

The Hessian soldiers were hired for their services. Over the course of the war, many came to support the colonists. By the end of the

A group of Hessian officers and soldiers relax outside a colonial tavern. Like the British, the German soldiers were well trained and supplied.

conflict some five thousand had quietly slipped away from their army to become Americans. Their officers, on the other hand, seemed to identify strongly with the British. This letter, identified only as being "From an Officer in New York," shows that point of view.

AT FIRST I WAS INCLINED to be favorable to the Americans. . . . But since I have had a chance to get closer acquainted with their history, their motives for the war, and their character as a whole, I have no further wishes for them. The most abominable trait in their make-up is ingratitude . . . let some one calculate for you . . . the unstinted care with which the mother country watched over its colonies from their origin; the severe and costly wars it fought . . . for the sake of this safety and quiet—whereby the Americans for the most part calmly looked on . . . and then, when it was asked, as was right and proper, that they should take upon their shoulders a part of these burdens . . . then the child rebelled against its mother.

—From Ray W. Pettengill, editor, Letters from America 1776–1779. *Port Washington, NY: Kennikat Press, 1924, pp. 228–229.*

Think about This

1. Why did this Hessian officer think the colonists were ungrateful?
2. If you were a Patriot, how might you answer this man?

Victory at Yorktown: A Firsthand Account

By the time of the last major battle of the Revolutionary War, American soldiers had all the experience, and assistance, they needed to defeat their enemies. Accompanied by the French soldiers under General Rochambeau, Washington's men lay siege to the British army at Yorktown. American doctor and officer James Thacher recorded the final attack and the surrender of the British army.

October 17, 1781

The whole peninsula trembles under the incessant thunderings of our infernal machines; we have leveled some of their works in ruins, and silenced their guns; they have almost ceased firing. We are so near as to have a distinct view of the dreadful havoc and destruction of their works, and even see the men in their lines tore to pieces by the bursting of our shells. . . .

October 19, 1781

It was about two o'clock when the captive army advanced through the line formed for their reception. Every eye was prepared to gaze on Lord Cornwallis, the object of peculiar interest and solicitude; but he disappointed our anxious expectations; pretending indisposition, he made General O'Hara his substitute as the leader of his army. This officer was followed by the conquered troops in a slow and solemn

The combined forces of General Washington and his French ally, General Rochambeau, forced a British surrender at Yorktown, Virginia, in the last major battle of the American Revolution.

step, with shouldered arms, colors cased, and drums beating a British march . . . their mortification could not be concealed. Some of the platoon officers appeared to be exceedingly chagrined when giving the word *"ground arms,"* and I am a witness that they performed this duty in a very unofficer-like manner; and that many of the soldiers manifested a *sullen temper,* throwing their arms on the pile with violence.

" Their mortification could not be concealed."

—From James Thacher, Military Journal during the American Revolutionary War. *Hartford, CT: Silas Andrus & Son, 1854, pp. 286, 289–290.*

Think about This

1. Why would the Americans have "solicitude," or concern, for Lord Cornwallis?
2. Why do you think Lord Cornwallis pretended he was sick and could not attend the surrender ceremony?
3. What does the writer mean by the expression a "very unofficer-like manner"?
4. If you were one of the British soldiers, how would you have conducted yourself at the ceremony?

Women supported the cause of independence as best they could. Here a Patriot offers money to an American officer to help buy needed supplies for the army.

Chapter 5

Women on the Home Front: Sacrifice and Service

THE ROLE OF WOMEN in the Revolutionary War was what one would expect for the time. They served their cause by sacrificing and by taking care of the needs of the soldiers. There were, as has often happened in conflicts, the few who actually managed to fight in the war, disguising themselves as young men. For the most part, however, a woman's role in the war was the traditional one—staying home and maintaining the farm or business until her husband returned.

Of course, staying at home sometimes meant the war came to you. Perhaps the worst situation for a woman was to be a Patriot in an area that was occupied by the British army. With her husband off fighting in the Continental Army, she would be constantly exposed to harassment from enemy soldiers. In New York City, Patriot women spent seven years living in enemy territory. Their service to the cause was probably as great as that of any soldier.

Other women found themselves evacuating their homes with the advance of the British army. They often were able to return within a fairly short period of time, only to find their houses and goods destroyed or stolen. Many of these women, without homes to go to or family to live with, simply followed their soldier-husbands around, living with the army.

Equally uprooted were the Loyalist wives living in what for them had become enemy territory. Some saw their husbands enlist to fight with the British, leaving them home to defend their property rights against people who had been their friends in the past. After the war, many Loyalists emigrated from the United States, moving to Britain or Canada to escape the new country that they had not chosen for themselves.

Uprooted in a different way were many of the wives of British and Hessian soldiers. These women had traveled across the ocean to spend the long years of the war with their husbands—a common practice at the time. For some, their visit to America might be spent as companion to a prisoner of war for years. Many had the additional burden of caring for children while adjusting to the hardships of life on the march with the army.

Women on both sides supported their cause by sewing uniforms and bandages and by nursing the wounded. Mostly, though, they focused on "keeping the home fires burning" while their men were at war.

A Chance to Help—The Call for Spinners

As war began, uniforms were among the first things the new American army needed. Women who answered the call to help would not only be aiding the war effort; they would also be acquiring jobs to help them support their families while their husbands were away. Advertisements in local newspapers were used to recruit women for this important work. In the following advertisement, the search is for "spinners"—people who prepared the cloth used to make the uniforms. The advertisement was posted in a Philadelphia newspaper in August 1775.

To the SPINNERS in this city, the suburbs, and country:—Your services are now wanted to promote the AMERICAN MANUFACTORY, at the corner of Market and Ninth streets, where cotton, wool, flax, &c., are delivered out; strangers, who apply, are desired to bring a few lines, by way of recommendation, from some respectable person in their neighborhood.

delivered out *the women would pick up materials and work at home*

One distinguishing characteristic of an excellent woman, as given by the wisest of men, is "That she seeketh wool and flax, and worketh willingly with her hands to the spindle, and her hands holdeth the distaff." In this time of public distress, you have now, each of you, an opportunity not only to help to sustain your families, but likewise to cast your mite into the treasury of the public good. The most feeble effort to help to save the state from ruin, when it is all you can do, is as the widow's mite, entitled to the same reward as they who, of their abundant abilities, have cast in much.

"You have now . . . an opportunity . . . to cast your mite into the treasury of the public good."

—*From* Pennsylvania Journal, *August 9, 1775. In Frank Moore,* Diary of the American Revolution from Newspapers and Original Documents, Vol. I. *New York: Charles Scribner, 1860, pp. 123–124.*

Think about This

1. What two inducements to women workers are offered in this advertisement?
2. Do you think women at the time would have been offered jobs like these if there were not a war?

Sympathy for Mrs. Washington

Martha Washington's letters were destroyed before her death. There are, however, some copies of letters written to her by others that have survived. Mercy Otis Warren, who was an acquaintance of Mrs. Washington, sent her the following letter of support in 1776. It speaks of Mrs. Washington's own sacrifice in her separation from her husband, but equally describes the fears of all of the Patriot women who sent their husbands off to possible death.

AMIDST THE PAIN and pomp of war, humanity recoils at the carnage of the species, yet if the blood of thousands must be the costly sacrifice, we hope heaven will accept the libation, and grant that freedom and virtue may soon be established on so permanent a base as to be fearless of the encroachments of future invaders. Then may the man dignified more by conscious worth than ever by the glory of conquest, return and taste the sweets of family felicity. . . . To the pain of a long separation from the friend and husband, you must my dear Madam when counting up the tedious hours of absence have suffered inexpressible anxiety for the safety of the

"You must my dear madam . . . have suffered inexpressible anxiety."

person, and for the honour of the commander of the united armies of America. Nor have you suffered alone, the prayers of the virtuous have accompanied each sigh, and the devout wishes of every lover of his country have breathed in unison with yours.

—*From letter of Mercy Otis Warren to Martha Washington, 1776.*
Mercy Otis Warren Papers. *Manuscript Division, Library of Congress.*

Think about This

1. What was Mercy Otis Warren's primary wish about the outcome of the war?
2. What did she believe Martha Washington's main concern to be as wife of the commander in chief?
3. Would you rather have been one of the men going off to fight or one of the women who stayed on the home front?

A Young Girl Encounters Battle

Sally Wister was a young Quaker girl living in Philadelphia during the Revolutionary War. The Quakers were pacifists and refused to support either side in the conflict. Many of them were Loyalist in their feelings. But Sally's family wished to see the Patriots win, and they fled the city when the British occupied it. Sally kept a journal of her adventures to share with a friend who stayed behind. This entry is for December 5, 1777.

OH, GRACIOUS! Debby, I am all alive with fear. The English have come out to attack (as we imagine) our army. They are on Chestnut Hill, our army three miles this side. What will become of us, only six miles distant?

Lydia Darrah, a Quaker, speaks to Colonel Craig, an aide to General Washington. Some Quakers, while officially remaining neutral, supported the American cause and offered vital information to the Continental Army on British troop movements.

We are in hourly expectation of an engagement. I fear we shall be in the midst of it. Heaven defend us from so dreadful a sight. The battle of Germantown, and the horrors of that day, are recent in my mind. It will be sufficiently dreadful if we are only in hearing of the firing, to think how many of our fellow-creatures are plung'd into the boundless ocean of eternity, few of them prepar'd to meet their fate. But they are summon'd before an all-merciful Judge, from whom they have a great deal to hope.

"What will become of us?"

—From Albert Cook Myers, editor, *Sally Wister's Journal*. Philadelphia: Ferris & Leach, 1902, pp. 108–109.

Think about This

1. What most frightened Sally about the possibility of the battle being nearby?
2. The Quakers refused to fight for either side because of their religion. Do you think they had a right not to defend their country (whether the United States or Great Britain) when everyone else was taking sides?
3. Are religious beliefs still a consideration in times of war today?

Living behind Enemy Lines: A Patriot

Lydia Minturn Post found herself behind enemy lines when the British occupied Long Island, New York. Her husband was an officer in Washington's army. She, left at home, found herself having to house Hessian soldiers. In this excerpt from her journal, she tells of frightening experiences in the area around her home in October 1776.

THE PATTISONS HAD a fine young heifer killed during the night. Some of the family heard the noise, but thought it most prudent not to make any resistance. The creature was drawn and quartered in the barn. What boldness!

Mrs. Clement, the wife of James Clement, was alone in the house with her children yesterday, about two miles hence, when an officer rode up, dismounted, and entered. He told her very civilly that he wanted supper for his company (about sixty men). She politely declined. He then began to insist, and at length said that they *should* come. Mrs. Clement replied that it was out of the question. She had nothing prepared; no person to assist her, and four little children to take care of. Still he rode off, saying they would be back in an hour for supper, and if she did not get it ready, she must take the consequences.

"She sat in fear and trembling."

She sat in fear and trembling through the hour, and her helplessness overcame her . . . they did not return.

—From Sidney Barclay [pseudonym], editor, Grace Barclay's *[Lydia Minturn Post]* Diary; or, Personal Recollection of the American Revolution. *New York: A.D.F. Randolph, 1866, pp. 34–36.*

Think about This

1. What do you think would be hardest about living behind enemy lines?

2. Why do you think the Pattisons did not go out and try to stop the British soldiers from killing their cow?

Living behind Enemy Lines: A Loyalist

There were women who lived behind enemy lines even in territory controlled by the Continental Army. These were the Loyalist women who stayed behind and tried to protect their property, waiting for the day when the rebellion would be put down and their lives could return to normal. Grace Galloway, a Loyalist wife who stayed behind in Philadelphia when her husband and daughter escaped to New York and then Britain, writes of her loneliness in this passage of a letter to her husband in 1780.

MY HEALTH HAS been Much impair'd for this Twelve Months but I try to Keep Up My Spirits, that I may one day see you & my Dearest Child again; but at Times I am very Apprehensive of it. My life I imagine will Now be of more importance to My Child than ever as her fortune Stands in a percarious [precarious] situation. . . . it would be a great relief to My Mind, to set my child above the insults of an Unthinking World. . . . There is Nothing so Disagreeable as writing Under Restraint so I shall say but little more but that I long to hear of your and Besteys Wellfare. . . . I will not Trouble You with My Afflictions but they are without bounds. . . . My Tenderest Care to My Darling Betsey.

under restraint *Mrs. Galloway refers to the fact that she cannot write freely because her letter might be intercepted*

—*From letter of Grace Galloway to Joseph Galloway, January 25, 1780.*Joseph Galloway Family Papers. *Manuscript Division, Library of Congress.*

Think about This

1. What was Grace Galloway's main concern as she wrote this letter?
2. Grace Galloway stayed behind to guard the family property. What do

you think this means the Galloways thought would be the result of the war? Why would she have stayed instead of her husband?

3. For a short time, Philadelphia was occupied by the British. As she wrote this letter, Grace was under American control. What kinds of "Afflictions" do you think she may be suffering?

Civilians under Attack

Eliza Wilkinson was a child when the British troops invading South Carolina drove her family from their home on three separate occasions. In spite of what must have been a frightening time in her life, she could look back on one of their narrow escapes in a lighthearted way.

I SHALL GIVE AN ACCOUNT of another run we had. Alas! poor we!—sure never were creatures so bandied about. One afternoon, my Father, taking a walk in his garden, observed a boat loaded with men, who, by their appearance, seemed to intend a visit; he was in great distress at the sight, having been used so ill by them, and they had sworn they would kill him yet . . . he was in a poor state of health . . . he could not survive it. He . . . got into a small canoe, and rowed up the creek . . . getting ashore at a neighboring plantation, he . . . sent off one of them to us . . . desiring us to quit the island directly, and come where he was. . . . It was about dusk when we evacuated the Island House, and had three long miles to walk. . . . Sometimes we would lose a shoe, which would stick fast under roots that ran across the path; at other times we stumbled over stumps, and ran against each other; for it was so dark we could not see many yards before us, and sometimes not at all when we got into a thick part of

"Alas! poor we!—sure never were creatures so bandied about."

the wood. . . . It grew late, and the darkness increased; every thing seemed awful about us, and, what increased the solemnity, the Birds of Minerva kept a continual hooting over our head, which were answered by their neighbors in the surrounding thickets; and, to complete the scene, the frogs joined their *melody*! and Mother's little girl (whom a servant carried in her arms) would scream out by way of *treble,* and I would as often lay hold of its mouth in order to stifle the cry. . . . Here was harmony, my dear! don't you admire it? We were serenaded in this *delightful* manner till we got near to the house, and then the dogs welcomed us with a howl.

—*From Eliza Longe Wilkinson,* Letters of Eliza Wilkinson, during the Invasion and Possession of Charleston, S.C., by the British in the Revolutionary War. *New York: S. Colman, 1839, pp. 72–75.*

THINK ABOUT THIS

1. Why do you think Eliza made light of her family's flight?
2. How do you think you would have reacted in Eliza's place?

A Hessian Wife on Traveling with the Army

Baroness de Riedesel

Baroness Friederika Charlotte de Riedesel was the wife of General Riedesel, leader of the Hessian troops who fought (and lost) with the British at the Battle of Saratoga in 1777. It was customary for officers' wives and families to travel with them when they were fighting overseas. The baroness made the trip with her

A group of Hessian soldiers on the march with their families. In Revolutionary War days, it was common for soldiers on both sides to travel with their wives and children.

three children, joined her husband in Canada, and stayed with him all the time that he was held captive after the battle, not returning to Hesse for several years. In this entry in the diary she promised to keep for her mother, the baroness describes her trip across the ocean with her children.

I DEPARTED, on the 14th of May 1776, at 5 o'clock in the morning, from Wolfenbütel, and notwithstanding my anxious desire to meet again with my husband, I could not but be alarmed at the difficulties of my undertaking, especially as, for some time, I had constantly been kept alive to the dangers to which I exposed myself. My eldest daughter, Gustava, was four years and nine months old; Frederica, my second daughter, was two years old; and Carolina was born but ten weeks before my departure. I needed all my courage and tenderness to keep my resolution of following my husband. Besides the perils of the sea, I was told that we were exposed to be eaten by the savages, and that people in America lived upon horse-flesh and cats. Yet all this frightened me less, than the idea of going into a country, with the language of which I was not conversant. I had, however, made up my mind; and the prospect of seeing my husband, and the consciousness of doing my duty, has preserved me during my whole voyage from despondency.

"I needed all my courage and tenderness to keep my resolution of following my husband."

—From Friederika Charlotte de Riedesel, Letters and Memoirs Relating to the War of American Independence and the Capture of the German Troops at Saratoga. *New York: G.C. Carvill, 1827, pp. 58–59.*

Think about This

1. Women were seen as the "weaker sex" at this time, unable to do anything on their own. Does the Baroness seem weak to you?
2. Why would it have bothered her most that she would be in a country where she did not speak the language?

Chapter 6

On the World Stage

MOST COLONIAL LEADERS HAD been appointed by the king of England and remained loyal to Britain when independence was declared. This meant that most of the people who found themselves running the government did not have experience as political leaders or as diplomats. Not only were they trying to manage a revolution, they were also trying to gain international support. It was yet another challenge they would face on the way to creating a new nation.

The first difficulty the government faced was convincing the British to recognize that the Americans were conducting the war as a separate nation rather than as disloyal subjects. There were rules of war, which all nations supposedly followed, concerning how captive soldiers and civilians were to be treated. These rules would not apply, however, if the conflict was considered an internal rebellion. By declaring independence, the colonies were telling the British and the rest of the world that they were not just a small group trying to overthrow their rulers. They were declaring themselves a nation, entitled to be treated as a nation.

The Americans needed foreign support to win their independence. General Washington was happy to greet French General Rochambeau and his troops when they arrived to assist in the fight.

With recognition of their status as citizens of a new nation, prisoners of war could not be tried and executed as traitors. They were to be treated humanely and could be released from captivity as part of prisoner exchanges. Wounded soldiers were to be cared for as one's own soldiers were cared for. Civilians were to be treated fairly, and their property could not be confiscated as long as they were not actively engaged in fighting. It was difficult for the Patriots to achieve this reasonably fair treatment when the British adamantly refused to accept that they were a legitimate nation.

If the British wouldn't acknowledge their independence (as was understandable since this was the very issue they were fighting about!), the next best situation was to have another major power recognize the United States as an independent country. That would force the British to treat the Americans as equals in battle, rather than as rebels, if only because they would be afraid to have one of the other major powers attack them.

Recognition by a major power was important for another reason. The Americans desperately needed foreign assistance. They needed money to pay and supply their army, and they needed foreign soldiers to join them in their fight.

Of course, the Americans could not really expect any European power to recognize them as an independent nation, at least not at first. The colonists were fighting against their king—but the European nations were also ruled by kings. Supporting such a revolution, the monarchs reasoned, might encourage their own people to rebel. The one thing the Americans could hope for was that many of these countries hated Great Britain and would be happy to see it fail. The Americans successfully exploited this animosity toward the British. Once the American armies proved that they were determined to achieve victory and could actually win a major battle (which they did at Saratoga), they received support from France (Britain's traditional rival) and several other European powers.

The intense international negotiations undertaken by Benjamin Franklin, John Adams, and Thomas Jefferson may have done as much to win the war as the fighting on the battlefields.

An Exchange of Letters between Enemies

It is not unusual during wartime for problems to arise in the treatment of civilians by enemy troops. Here we have an exchange of letters between General Parsons of the Continental Army and British General William Tryon about an incident in which a Patriot family was harassed. General Parsons is protesting a situation that he feels goes beyond the allowable treatment of civilians during wartime.

November 16, 1777

On the 15th of Nov. Capt. Emmerick came with a Flagg from the Enemy to Tarry Town . . . to bring Letters to Gen'l Putnam. But in Reality to discover the Situation & Strength of Our Guards as he the next Day declared. On Monday, ye 17th Captains Emmerick & Barns with 100 Men were sent out with Orders to burn Tarry Town & the Dwelling Houses of Peter & Cornelius Vantassel . . . they came to Vantassels about 1 o'Clock Tuesday morning, fird [fired] the House & turnd the Family out of the House half Naked & the cloths they caught in their Hands forceably wrested from them & threw into the Flames. Vantassel had not time to put on any part of his Clothing but

Patriots in British-held areas sometimes had alarming experiences with enemy soldiers.

his Breeches & Stockings, in this Situation, they put an Halter about his Neck & led him to Kingsbridge about Ten Miles in one of the Severest Nights we have had: the Old Man before he had reachd halfwy Distance had almost perishd with the Cold, his Feet with the Ice & frozen Ground were so torn that the Blood markd every Step. . . . These Facts I collected from Persons who were Eye Witnesses to the Transactions at different Times on their Way to the Enemies Lines.

S. H. Parsons

". . . his Feet with the Ice & frozen Ground were so torn that the Blood markd every Step."

transactions
Events

This is the response to General Parson from General Tryon.

King's Bridge Camp 23rd Nov 1777

Sir

Could I possibly conceive myself accountable to any Revolted Subject of the King of Great Britain, I might answer your letter received by the flag of Truce yesterday respecting the conduct of the Party under Captn Emmericks command upon the taking of Peter and Cornelius Vantassel; I have however candor enough to assure you, as much as I abhor every principle of Inhumanity or ungenerous Conduct, I should, were I in more authority, Burn every Committee Man's House within my reach, as I deem those Agents the wicked instruments of the continued Calamities of this Country; And in Order the sooner to purge this Colony of them, I am willing to give Twenty Silver Dollars for every Acting Committee Man who shall be delivered up to the King's troops; I guess before the end of the next Campaign they will be torn to pieces by their own countrymen whom they have forcibly dragged; in opposition to their Principles and Duty . . . to take up Arms against their Lawfull Sovereign, and compelled them to Exchange their happy constitution for Paper, Rags, Anarchy and Distress . . .

I am Sir,
Your Obedt Servt
Wm Tryon

—*From the* Henley Smith Collection *(Items 1412 and 1413). Manuscript Division, Library of Congress.*

Think about This

1. Why do you think there are rules of war for incidents like this? Why not just attack the enemy in response?
2. Contrast the two letters. Does one seem more professional than the other?

Looking for Allies: An American in Paris Speculates

The Patriots long knew that their most likely source of foreign support would be France. Britain's longtime rival, they thought, would be happy to see her humiliated by her colonies. As early as 1775, there was speculation in the colonial newspapers as to whether the French would acknowledge the colonies as a nation if they declared independence. This example is from the *Gaines' Mercury* of July 10, 1775.

A CORRESPONDENT at Paris, says:—"I find the French are extremely attentive to our American politics, and to a man, strongly in favor of us. Whether mostly from ill-will to Britain, or friendship to the colonies, may be matter of doubt; but they profess it to be upon a principle of humanity, and a regard to the natural rights of mankind. They say that the Americans will be either revered or detested by all Europe, according to their conduct at the approaching crisis. They will have no middle character; for in proportion as their virtue and perseverance will render them a glorious [people], their tame submission will make them a despicable people."

"I find the French are extremely attentive to our American politics. . . . Whether mostly from ill-will to Britain, or friendship to the colonies, may be a matter of doubt."

—*From* Gaines' Mercury, *July 10, 1775. In Frank Moore,* Diary of the American Revolution from Newspapers and Original Documents, Vol. I. *New York: Charles Scribner, 1860, p. 73.*

THINK ABOUT THIS

1. What reasons did the writer give for why the French are likely to support the Americans?
2. Why would Americans be detested if they submitted to Great Britain?

John Hancock's Instructions to Benjamin Franklin

Benjamin Franklin was chosen as the ambassador to France and given the difficult task of negotiating a treaty with the French to assist the colonists in their fight. From Franklin's papers, we have a

Benjamin Franklin was enormously popular at the French court. He won much support for the American cause among French nobles, who did not see at the time that their enthusiasm for democracy would help bring about their own downfall.

copy of the secret instructions given to him by John Hancock, president of the Continental Congress.

THERE IS DELIVERED TO YOU herewith a plan of a treaty with his most Christian majesty of France . . . you are hereby instructed to use every means in your power for concluding it. . . . If you shall find that to be impracticable, you are hereby authorized to relax the demands of the United States. . . . You will solicit the Court of France for an immediate supply of twenty or thirty thousand muskets and bayonets, and a large supply of ammunition and brass fieldpieces [cannons], to be sent under convoy by France. . . . It is highly probable that France means not to let the United States sink in the present contest. But as the difficulty of obtaining true accounts of our condition may cause an opinion to be entertained that we are able to support the war on our own strength and resources longer than, in fact, we can do, it will be proper for you to press for an immediate and explicit declaration of France in our favor, upon a suggestion that a reunion with Great Britain may be the consequence of a delay.

"It is highly probable that France means not to let the United States sink in the present contest."

—*From Edward E. Hale,* Franklin in France, From Original Documents, Part I. *Boston: Roberts Brothers, 1888, pp. 61–64.*

Think about This

1. What does Congress make as Franklin's first priority?
2. Why would the threat of the colonies rejoining Great Britain be something the French would oppose?

The Marquis Speaks of His Admiration for the Americans

The Marquis de Lafayette is perhaps the most famous of the allies who came to help the Americans win their independence from Britain. In some ways it was natural for him to want to help, for the British and French were longtime enemies. But the marquis seemed to be fighting for the ideals of the revolution. Interestingly enough, those same ideals would tear France apart in a few years, destroying many of the noble class to which the Marquis de Lafayette belonged.

In the following letter, the marquis is writing to the Continental Congress in thanks for praise he received from its members in a resolution passed on September 9, 1778.

I HAVE RECEIVED your favour of the 13th instant, acquainting me with the honor Congress has been pleased to confer on me, by their most generous resolve. Whatever pride such approbation may justly give me, I am not less affected by the feelings of gratitude, and that satisfaction of thinking my endeavors were ever looked upon as useful in the cause in which my heart is so deeply interested. Be so good, Sir, as to present to Congress, my plain and hearty thanks. . . . The moment I heard of America I loved her; the moment I knew she was fighting for liberty I burnt with a desire of bleeding for her; and the moment I shall be able to serve her, at any time, or in any part of the world, will be the happiest of my life. I never so much as wished for occasions of deserving those obliging sentiments I am honored with by these

instant
the current month, in this case, September

"The moment I heard of America I loved her."

The Marquis de Lafayette was one of the earliest French supporters of the American Revolution. He offered his services even before his government had declared its support.

States, and their representatives; and that so flattering confidence as they have been pleased to put in me, filled my heart with the warmest acknowledgments, and most eternal affection.

—From Frederick Butler, Memoirs of the Marquis de Lafayette. *Wethersfield, CT: Deming & Francis, 1825, pp. 25–26.*

THINK ABOUT THIS

What reason does Lafayette give for wanting to fight for America?

Chapter 7

To Pay the Price

SOLDIERS PAY THE PRICE of war—as prisoners, as wounded or sick men, or in death. When a war is over these human casualities are the numbers we add up to determine its cost.

The treatment of prisoners of war was one of the most controversial aspects of the Revolutionary War. It could range from the relatively civilized (in the case of the Hessians taken prisoner by the Americans after the surrender at Saratoga) to the truly brutal (the death of about half of the soldiers of the Continental Army captured at the Battle of Fort Washington and housed on British prison ships). For the American soldiers, the prospect of being captured was a terrible one, as we shall read.

Equally unpleasant was the prospect of disease or wounds. The state of medicine at the time seems barbaric to us now. Disease caused seven out of every eight deaths in the Revolutionary War. Soldiers arriving in camp suffered initially from major outbreaks of smallpox. Those that survived then faced the routine camp diseases caused by the lack of cleanliness, the poor quality of the food and drinking water, and the crowded and unsanitary living conditions.

Historical paintings often romanticize war. This engraving of the June 1778 Battle of Monmouth, in New Jersey, is more realistic than many.

Dysentery, typhoid fever (called camp fever, jail fever, or putrid fever), ague (malaria), and scurvy were common.

Doctors knew little about the causes of disease, although they tried desperately to keep the armies healthy. Most treatment involved some form of bleeding the patient, combined with the use of purgatives and laxatives to rid the body of what were called "ill humors," which supposedly caused disease. These "treatments" probably made the patients weaker, sapping their own natural mechanisms for fighting disease.

The treatment of wounds was equally primitive. There was no anesthesia. A dose of rum or whiskey and a lead bullet to bite on provided all the pain relief a soldier might receive. Doctors were unaware of the need to keep wounds clean, and infection was a frequent problem. Perhaps the most amazing thing is that so many soldiers survived the war and its medical treatment.

Death was, of course, the highest price a soldier might pay. Most soldiers were buried in mass graves after a battle. There are many accounts of bodies being quickly buried only to surface several weeks later as rain and erosion washed away their shallow coverings of dirt. Officers were more likely to be buried in individual graves and have their deaths noted and memorialized. The numbers of soldiers killed in the fighting over the eight years of the war is unknown. Some estimates say there were seven thousand to nine thousand American deaths in battle, and more than eight thousand deaths among the American prisoners of war. The British had more than ten thousand battle deaths. The blood of both sides paid for the freedom of the new nation.

The British prison ship *Jersey*, anchored off New York City

An Account of Life Aboard British Prison Ships

One of the true horrors of the Revolutionary War was the treatment of prisoners of war by the British. The following account appeared in an American newspaper after the British released some prisoners in 1777. Half of the prisoners had died while in British custody.

AS SOON AS THEY WERE taken they were robbed . . . and many were stripped almost naked of their clothes. Especially those who had good clothes, were stripped at once, being told that *such clothes were too good for rebels.* Thus deprived of their clothes and baggage they were unable to shift even their linen, and were obliged to wear the same shirts for even three or four months together, whereby they became extremely nasty; and this of itself was sufficient to bring on them many mortal diseases.

linen
underclothes

"What was given them for three days was not enough for one day."

After they were taken, they were in the first place put on board the ships and thrust down into the hold, where not a breath of fresh air could be obtained and they were nearly suffocated for want of air. . . .

They suffered extremely for want of provisions. . . . What was given them for three days was not enough for one day; and in some

The conditions on the British prison ships were truly horrible and resulted in the deaths of half of the Americans imprisoned on them.

instances, they went for three days without a single mouthful of food of any sort. . . .

The water allowed them was so brackish and withal nasty, that they could not drink it, till reduced to extremity [until they were so thirsty they had to drink it]. Nor did they let them have a sufficiency even of such water as this.

When winter came on our people suffered extremely for want of fire and clothes to keep them warm. . . . Nor had they a single blanket or any bedding, not even straw, allowed them till a little before Christmas.

At the time those were taken on Long Island, a considerable part of them were sick of the dysentery, and with this distemper on them were first crowded on board the ships, afterwards in the churches in

New York, three, four, or five hundred together, without any blankets, or any thing for even the sick to lie upon. . . . In this situation that contagious distemper soon communicated from the sick to the well. . . . Of this distemper numbers died daily, and many others, by their confinement and the sultry season, contracted fevers and died of them . . . they had no medicines . . . were not so much as visited by the physician.

—*From* Freeman's Journal, *February 18, 1777. In Frank Moore,* Diary of the American Revolution from Newspapers and Original Documents, Vol. I. *New York: Charles Scribner, 1860, pp. 374–376.*

Think about This

1. Which of the conditions mentioned would have caused the prisoners to become ill?
2. Why do you think the British broke the rules of war in the case of the captured Americans?

Battling Disease: A German Doctor Describes a Different Kind of War

The British and Hessian soldiers were well trained and equipped, but they were not prepared for the extreme temperatures of the American climate. In the following account, a German doctor describes the impact some very hot weather had on the soldiers' ability to fight.

THE BATTLE NEAR MONMOUTH, on June 28, 1778, was remarkable from one circumstance which has not its parallel in the history of the

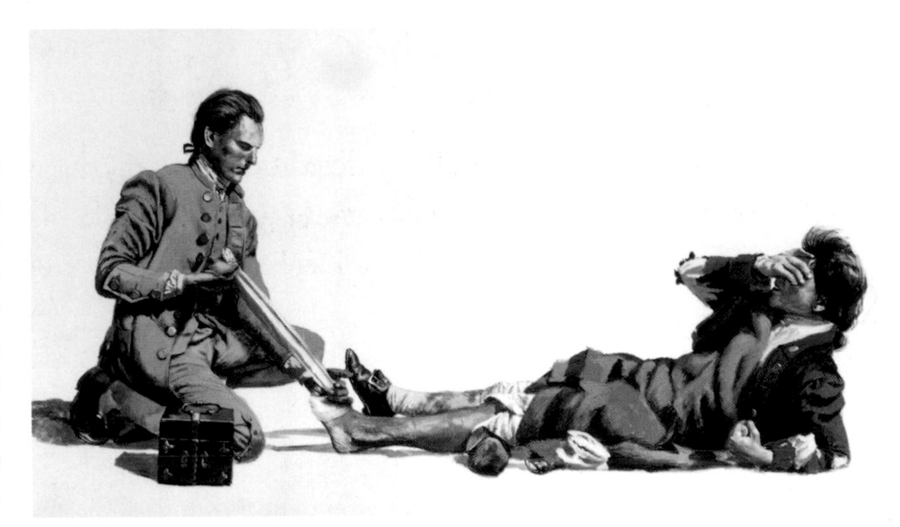

Doctors did their best to care for the wounded and sick with what materials they could find. Here a physician is using tent cloth to bandage a frostbitten foot.

New World; without receiving a wound, fifty-nine men fell on our side solely from the extraordinary heat and fatigue of the day; and many on the side of the rebels succumbed to the same causes, in spite of the men being more accustomed to the climate. . . . Our troops arrived here in July. From that time till October most of our men were, one after another, in the hospitals of New York, or in the regimental hospitals on Staaten-Eyland or at Harlem; there were very few who escaped without an attack of dysentery or fever.

". . . without receiving a wound, fifty-nine men fell on our side solely from the extraordinary heat and fatigue of the day."

—*From Johann David Schoepff,* The Climate and Diseases of America. *Boston: H. O. Houghton, 1875, pp. 12, 22.*

Think about This

Could the doctors have done anything to prepare the soldiers for the conditions in America?

What Doctors Didn't Know: Advice from a Revolutionary War Medical Textbook

Soldiers on both sides of the conflict suffered from disease. But what they feared more was infection from battle wounds. Doctors had only limited knowledge about germs. Here is an excerpt from a medical textbook of the day.

MANY WOUNDS ALSO in themselves not mortal, may be rendered so by neglect or erroneous treatment; this frequently happens to soldiers and seamen in the day of battle, when the multiplicity of cases prevents the Surgeons from paying a proper attention to all,—hence many die of haemorrhages which might have been stopped. . . . Errors in practice have the same fatal consequence. . . .

About the fourth day, sooner or later, according to the age of the patient and heat of the weather, a white, pinguious, equal matter, called pus, is generated in the wound; and this produces very happy effects, by separating the lacerated vessels and extravasated fluids from the sound parts which then grow up a-fresh,—hence laudable pus is esteemed by Surgeons the best of signs.

haemorrhages *heavy, uncontrolled bleeding*

pinguious *yellowish, fatty substance found in wounds*

equal *unvaried in appearance, regular*

extravasated *liquids that have been forced out of where they belong in the body*

—From Dr. John Jones, Plain Consise Practical Remarks on the Treatment of Wounds and Fractures. *Philadelphia: Robert Bell, 1776, pp. 14–16.*

Think about This

1. This was a very modern book at the time. What do you think of the doctor's medical advice?
2. What kinds of things about medicine do we know now that might have helped these doctors?

The "great and good" Dr. Warren. His death in the Battle of Bunker Hill made him a lasting symbol of patriotism.

Remembering a Patriot

Dr. Joseph Warren was a well-known and popular Massachusetts Patriot. He died at the Battle of Bunker Hill, the first major battle of the Revolutionary War, and was remembered as a symbol of Patriotic resistance to British tyranny. His biographer recorded the way people felt when they first learned of his death.

The general grief attests the hold which he had on the affections of his countrymen. I select a few independent contemporary expressions. . . . "We have yet about sixty or seventy killed or missing; but—among these is—what shall I say? how shall I write the name of our worthy friend, the great and good Dr. Warren. The tears of multitudes pay tribute to his memory. Not all the havoc and devastation they [the British] have made has wounded me like the death of Warren. We want him in the senate; we want him in his profession; we want him in the field. We mourn for the citizen, the senator, the physician, and the warrior. When he fell, liberty wept. He closed a life of glory in a glorious death; and heaven never received the spirit of a purer patriot. . . . He fell in the glorious struggle for public liberty."

". . . heaven never received the spirit of a purer patriot."

—*From Richard Frothingham,* Life and Times of Joseph Warren. *Boston: Little, Brown, & Company, 1865, pp. 520–521.*

Think about This

1. Why do you think there was such an outpouring of grief for Dr. Warren?
2. Name some famous people of your time who have died. How were they memorialized?

Chapter 8

Victory and Defeat

THE WAR THAT BEGAN in April 1775 with shots fired at Lexington and Concord finally ended with the evacuation of British troops from New York City on November 25, 1783. The major fighting had ended two years earlier when the British army, under General Cornwallis, surrendered to the American army under George Washington at Yorktown.

The colonies were finally free. There would be several years of uncertainty as they developed their own form of government. When the U.S. Constitution was approved in 1788, the first president of the United States of America would have a familiar name. George Washington, who had retired to his home at Mount Vernon, Virginia, would again accept his country's call and become its first president. John Adams, who had worked so hard as a member of the Continental Congress and who had served as the first ambassador to Great Britain after the war, was elected vice president.

For the Patriots, there were, of course, losses to go along with

In November 1783, the last of the British soldiers evacuated the city of New York, finally bringing the war to a close.

their victories. Many supporters had died. Others would have to live with the effects of imprisonment or injuries sustained in battle. Many families had lost husbands and fathers. Financially, the new country would need a long time to recover.

Those who had supported the king were faced with an interesting choice. Some Loyalists chose to remain and accept the reality of living in the new nation. More than 100,000 left, moving to Nova Scotia in Canada, to other British colonies, or to Great Britain itself. They incurred financial losses from which they never fully recovered as they left behind their businesses, homes, and belongings.

The British soldiers returned home. So did their Hessian allies, although not all of them. About five thousand Hessian soldiers quietly deserted and became Americans. The French soldiers also returned home. Their own history as a nation would be turbulent in the coming years as the French populace, in turn, revolted against their king. The French Revolution was inspired in part by the success of the American Revolution and its commitment to the ideals of freedom and democracy. Ironically, the French monarchy also suffered from indebtedness incurred in part because of all of the financial support it provided to the Americans.

This most amazing war was over. The colonies were independent. The British king and government had to face the humiliation of receiving an American ambassador as a representative of a free and equal nation. The British empire would never be the same. As for the Americans, their long and glorious history as a republic was just beginning.

Celebrating Victory at Yorktown: A Newspaper Account

The defeat and surrender of General Cornwallis's army at Yorktown, Virginia, in 1781 was greeted throughout the new country with great joy. It was not known at the time that it would be the decisive battle leading to a peace treaty two years later. But everyone knew it was important. Here is one newspaper account of a celebration marking the event.

October 28.—Yesterday the great and important event of the surrender of Lord Cornwallis and his whole army, to the combined forces commanded by his Excellency GENERAL WASHINGTON, was celebrated at Trenton, in New Jersey, with every mark of joy and festivity. The day was ushered in with the beating of drums, and the American colors were displayed in various parts of the town. . . .

At noon a proper discharge of cannon was fired by the corps of artillery belonging to the town, in the presence of the Governor, General Dickinson, the members of the Legislature, and the gentlemen of the town and neighborhood, assembled on the common.

At three in the afternoon the company repaired to an elegant entertainment, at which the following toasts were drank, and severally accompanied with a discharge of artillery. . . .

Every thing was conducted with the greatest good order and propriety, and we mention it with pleasure, that not the least disturbance or irregularity happened during the whole festivity.

—*From* New Jersey Gazette, *October 31, 1781. In Frank Moore,* Diary of the American Revolution from Newspapers and Original Documents, Vol. II. *New York: Charles Scribner, 1860, pp. 519–521.*

Think about This

1. Do you think any women were in attendance at this celebration? If no, why not? If yes, why were they not mentioned in the newspaper account?
2. Why kind of disturbance or irregularity might the town have been afraid of?

A British General Admits Defeat

Lord Cornwallis faced the humiliating task of surrendering his army to George Washington. Angered to be forced to submit, he refused to attend the surrender ceremony, sending his second in command to present his sword, the accepted symbol of admission of defeat. His second then compounded the insult by attempting to surrender to the French officers on the field, rather than to the "Colonials." With the surrender over, Cornwallis sent his men the following gracious message:

"Lord Cornwallis cannot sufficiently express his gratitude to the Officers & Soldiers of the Army."

Hquarters, York, 19th Octr 1781

Lord Cornwallis cannot sufficiently express his gratitude to the Officers & Soldiers of the Army for their good conduct on any occasion since he has had the honor to command them but particularly for their extraordinary Courage & perseverance in the defense of this Post, he sincerely laments that their efforts have not been successful, but the Powerfull Artillery which was opposed to them could not be resisted & the blood of the bravest men would have been shed in vain—Lord Cornwallis did every thing in his power to procure for the Soldiers the terms of being sent to Europe; since those could not be obtained he

Lord Cornwallis sent his second in command to the surrender ceremony rather than face his defeat by the Americans.

has taken every means to secure to them good treatment during their Captivity; & will pay the greatest Attention to their being constantly supplied with Necessaries until their Liberty can be procured.

—*From* Orderly Book of the British Army, May 23–Oct. 22, 1781. *Manuscript Division, Library of Congress.*

Think about This

1. What did Cornwallis promise to the soldiers since he failed to negotiate their return home?
2. Why do you think the Americans would not release the British soldiers?

A Taunting Song Commemorates Victory

Songs were popular among the soldiers, and they often celebrated victories by singing new words to an old song. This happened after Cornwallis's surrender at Yorktown. The following lyrics were written to the song "Maggie Lauder," which had been popular with both armies.

CORNWALLIS BERGOYNED
When British troops first landed here,
With Howe commander o'er them,
They thought they'd make us quake for fear,
And carry all before them;
With thirty thousand men or more,
And she without assistance,
America must needs give o'er,
And make no more resistance.

But Washington, her glorious son,
Of British hosts the terror,
Soon, by repeated overthrows,
Convinc'd them of their error;
Let Princeton, and let Trenton tell,
What gallant deeds he's done, sir,
And Monmouth's plains where hundreds fell,
And thousands more have run, sir.

Major General Benjamin Lincoln accepts the British surrender at Yorktown on October 19, 1781.

Cornwallis, too, when he approach'd
Virginia's old dominion,
Thought he would soon her conqu'ror be;
And so was North's opinion.
From State to State with rapid stride,
His troops had march'd before, sir,
Till quite elate with martial pride,
He thought all dangers o'er, sir.

But our allies, to his surprise,
The Chesapeake had enter'd;

And now too late, he curs'd his fate,
And wish'd he ne'er had ventur'd,
For Washington no sooner knew
The visit he had paid her,
Then to his parent State he flew,
To crush the bold invader.

"Then let us toast America!"

When he sat down before the town,
His Lordship soon surrender'd;
His martial pride he laid aside,
And cas'd the British standard;
Gods! how this stroke will North provoke,
And all his thoughts confuse, sir!
And how the Peers with hang their ears,
When first they hear the news, sir.

Be peace, this glorious end of war,
By this event effected;
And be the name of Washington,
To latest times respected;
Then let us toast America,
And France in union with her;
And may Great Britain rue the day
Her hostile bands came hither.

—*From Frank Moore,* Songs and Ballads of the American Revolution. *New York: D. Appleton & Company, 1856, pp. 367–369.*

Think about This

1. Who is given credit for winning the war in this song?
2. What failing best describes the British leaders?
3. Do we still write new verses to songs to remember events?

The Ultimate Success—The American Ambassador Visits the King

With American victory came a particularly satisfying moment when the first ambassador of the new nation, John Adams, was received by the king and queen of England. Abigail Adams, his wife, describes the ceremony in a letter to her sister.

THE TORY VENOM has begun to spit itself forth in the public papers, as I expected, bursting with envy that an American Minister should be received here with the same marks of attention, politeness, and civility, which are shown to the ministers of any other power. . . . The answer of his Majesty was much longer; but I am not at liberty to say more respecting it, than that it was civil and polite, and that his Majesty said he was glad the choice of his country had fallen upon him [Abigail's husband, John Adams]. . . . Congratulate me, my dear sister, it is over. . . . At two o'clock went to the circle, which is in the drawing-room of the Queen. . . . The King is a personable man. . . . When he came to me, Lord Onslow said, "Mrs. Adams;" upon which I drew off my right-hand glove, and his Majesty saluted my left cheek; then asked me if I had taken a walk today. I could have told his Majesty that I had been all the morning preparing to wait upon him. . . . The Queen was evidently embarrassed when I was presented to her. I had disagreeable feelings too. . . . As to the ladies of the Court, rank and title may compensate for want of personal charms; but they are, in general, very plain, ill-shaped, and ugly; but don't you tell anybody that I say so. . . . The Tories are very free with their compliments. Scarcely a paper escapes

"The Tory venom has begun to spit itself forth in the public papers."

Abigail Adams, wife of the first U.S. ambassador to Great Britain, found the English people still angry at their loss to the Americans.

John Adams, representative from the new republic, received a "civil and polite" reception from his majesty, the king.

without some scurrility. We bear it with silent contempt; having met a polite reception from the Court, it bites them like a serpent, and stings them like an adder.

—From Letter of Abigail Adams to Mary Cranch, London, 24 June 1785.
In Charles Frances Adams, editor, Letters of Mrs. Adams.
Boston: Wilkins, Carter, and Company, 1848, pp. 253, 256–258.

Think about This

1. What opinion did Mrs. Adams form of King George III?
2. How did the Adamses respond to the anti-Americanism of the Tories?
3. Do you think Mrs. Adams enjoyed her experience of being presented at court?

Time Line

APRIL 19, 1775
Battle of Lexington and Concord

JUNE 17, 1775
Battle of Bunker Hill

MARCH 17, 1776
Evacuation of Boston by the British

JULY 1776
British begin occupation of New York City

JULY 4, 1776
Declaration of Independence

DECEMBER 26, 1776
Battle of Trenton (New Jersey)

SEPTEMBER 26, 1777
British begin occupation of Philadelphia

OCTOBER 7, 1777
Battle of Saratoga (New York)

JUNE 1778
British evacuate Philadelphia

JUNE 28, 1778
Battle of Monmouth Courthouse (New Jersey)

AUGUST 23, 17
Battle of Savan (Georgia)

APRIL–MAY 1780

Battle of Charleston (South Carolina)

SEPTEMBER 28–OCTOBER 19,1781

Battle of Yorktown; British surrender one-quarter of their troops

NOVEMBER 18, 1781

British evacuate Wilmington (North Carolina)

JULY 11, 1782

Battle of Monmouth Courthouse (New Jersey)

DECEMBER 14, 1782

British evacuate Charleston

SEPTEMBER 3, 1783

Peace treaty signed between British and Americans

NOVEMBER 25, 1783

Last British troops on American soil begin evacuation of New York City and Long Island

Glossary

colony a territory that is ruled by another country

commissary general the person in charge of obtaining food and supplies for soldiers

Continental Army the army authorized by the Second Continental Congress to fight the British

Continental Congress a gathering of representatives from each of the colonies that acted as a government on their behalf during and after the American Revolution

deposition a statement made under oath and recorded in writing about an event one has witnessed

duties fees assessed on certain goods arriving into a country; in the American colonies, duties were charged on items such as paper, tea, and glass

dysentery severe diarrhea caused by impure food or water

liberty pole a pole erected in a town green, symbolizing that the people were in support of the Revolution

militia local military units, usually formed by towns or counties for quick self-defense

negotiation a process in which agreement is sought that gives both sides some satisfaction

neutral refusing to take sides in a conflict

occupation control of an area by the military force of an enemy

pacifist one who believes war is wrong

ration the food allowance that a soldier receives each day

scurvy a disease common in soldiers and seamen during the Revolutionary War, caused by a lack of vitamin C, which is found in fresh vegetables and fruits

self-determination the process by which the colonies could govern themselves; the colonies were seeking the right to have more say in their governance rather than be subject to the laws of the British Parliament

snipers soldiers who shoot at people from a hiding place

stalemate a time during a conflict in which neither party can advance

Tory the conservative political party in England, which was opposed to democratic ideals; also a name used to refer to Loyalists in the colonies

trebuchet a military machine used to hurl large objects such as rocks

unalienable something that cannot be taken away

To Find Out More

BOOKS

Beller, Susan Provost. *Revolutionary War (Letters from the Homefront).* New York: Marshall Cavendish, 2002.

Bliven, Bruce. *The American Revolution.* New York: Random House, 1987.

Dolan, Edward F. *The American Revolution: How We Fought the War of Independence.* Brookfield, CT: Millbrook Press, 1995.

Egger-Bovet, Howard. *Book of the American Revolution.* Boston: Little, Brown & Company, 1994.

Gay, Kathlyn. *Revolutionary War: Voices from the Past.* Brookfield, CT: Twenty-First Century Books, 1995.

Grant, R. G. *The American Revolution (Revolution!)* Stamford, CT: Thomson Learning, 1995.

Kent, Deborah. *The American Revolution: "Give Me Liberty, or Give Me Death."* Springfield, NJ: Enslow Publishers, 1994.

Marrin, Albert. *The War for Independence: The Story of the American Revolution.* New York: Atheneum, 1988.

Meyeroff, Stephen. *The Call for Independence: The Story of the American Revolution and Its Cause.* Claremont, CA: Oak Tree Publishing, 1996.

Moore, Kay. *If You Lived at the Time of the American Revolution.* New York: Scholastic Press, 1998.

Steins, Richard. *A Nation Is Born: Rebellion and Independence in America, 1700–1820.* Brookfield, CT: Twenty-First Century Books, 1993.

Weber, Michael. *The American Revolution.* Chatham, NJ: Raintree/Steck Vaughn, 2000.

PLACES TO VISIT

Boston National Historical Park, Massachusetts

Colonial National Historical Park (includes Yorktown battlefield), Virginia

Cowpens National Battlefield, South Carolina

Fort Ticonderoga, New York

Guilford Courthouse National Military Park, North Carolina

Independence National Historical Park, Philadelphia, Pennsylvania

Kings Mountain National Military Park, South Carolina

Minute Man National Historical Park (includes Lexington and Concord), Massachusetts

Moores Creek National Battlefield, South Carolina

Morristown National Historical Park, New Jersey

Mount Independence Historic Site, Vermont

Saratoga National Historical Park, New York

Valley Forge National Historical Park, Pennsylvania

VIDEOS

Liberty—The American Revolution. PBS Home Video, 1998.

The Crossing. A&E, 2000.

WEBSITES

The websites listed here were in existence in 2000–2001 when this book was being written. Their names or locations may have changed since then.

In general, when using the Internet to do research on a history topic, you should use caution. You will find numerous websites that are very attractive to look at and appear to be professional in format. Proceed with caution, however. Many, even the best ones, contain errors. Some websites even insert disclaimers or warnings about mistakes that may have made their way into the site. In the case of primary sources, the builders of the website often transcribe previously published material, good or bad, accurate or inaccurate. Therefore, you have to judge the content of *all* websites. This requires a critical eye.

A good rule for using the Internet as a resource is always to compare what you find in websites to several other sources such as librarian- or teacher-recommended reference works and major works of scholarship. By doing this, you will discover the myriad versions of history that exist.

www.earlyamerica.com is the home page of Archiving Early America: Historic Documents from 18th-Century America. This is a great source for pamphlets, speeches, and other primary source material for colonial America.

www.pbs.org/ktca/liberty/chronicle is the URL for Liberty: Chronicle of the Revolution. This site provides excellent topical coverage of all aspects of the American Revolution, including battles, political events, and the lives of the common people of the time.

www.nara.gov is the home page for the National Archives. At its Online Exhibit Hall, you can see original copies of the Declaration of Independence and the U.S. Constitution. This site also connects to NAIL, the National Archives site that contains copies of materials from their collections.

http://lcweb.loc.gov/spcoll/clist18.html is the URL for the Special Collections of the Library of Congress: 18th Century. This page features descriptions of materials available through the Library of Congress on the Revolutionary War and the colonial period.

www.si.umich.edu/SPIES/index.html is the URL for Spy Letters of the American Revolution, Clements Library, University of Michigan. This page provides digital reproductions of actual letters from the Revolutionary War period with transcriptions and context information.

Index

Page numbers for illustrations are in boldface

ABOUT THE AUTHOR

"I grew up in New England and found learning about the Revolutionary War in Massachusetts boring until I discovered Abigail Adams, the wife of John Adams, one of the founding fathers. Here she was, at a time when men decided everything, raising and teaching their children, being a more successful farmer than her husband had been, entertaining visitors like George Washington, and writing hundreds of letters describing events from the perspective of someone waiting at home. She absolutely fascinated me, and through her I came to appreciate every aspect of the Revolutionary War."

Susan Provost Beller is the author of thirteen history books for young readers and teaches teachers how to use primary sources and historic sites to make history more interesting for their students. She lives with her husband, Michael, in Vermont. She and her husband spend their free travel time visiting Revolutionary War and Civil War sites in the United States and ancient Roman sites in Europe. With their three children, Michael, Jennifer, and Sean, now grown and two grandchildren too young to take along on visits to historic sites, they can enjoy the visits without listening to Sean complain, "Just once I'd like to go on a vacation where I don't learn anything."